EQUALITY DEFERRED

RACE, ETHNICITY, AND IMMIGRATION IN AMERICA SINCE 1945

James S. Olson
Sam Houston State University

D0218146

THOMSON
™
WADSWORTH

Australia • Canada • Mexico • Singapore • Spain
United Kingdom • United States

WADSWORTH

THOMSON LEARNING ™

Publisher, History: Clark Baxter
Development Editor: Sue Gleson
Assistant Editor: Julie Iannacchino
Editorial Assistant: Jonathan Katz
Technology Project Manager: Jennifer Ellis
Marketing Manager: Caroline Croley
Marketing Assistant: Mary Ho
Advertising Project Manager: Brian Chaffee
Project Manager, Editorial Production:
Matt Ballantyne
Print/Media Buyer: Robert King

Permissions Editor: Bob Kauser
Production Service: Shepherd, Inc.
Photo Researcher: Meyers Photo-Art
Copy Editor: Jennifer Gordon
Proofreader: Jennifer Chambliss
Indexer: Susan Coerr
Cover Designer: Preston Thomas
Cover Image: © Bettmann/Corbis
Compositor: Shepherd, Inc.
Text and Cover Printer: Transcontinental
Printing

For more information about our products, contact us at:
Thomson Learning Academic Resource Center
1-800-423-0563
For permission to use material from this text, contact us by:
Phone: 1-800-730-2214
Fax: 1-800-730-2215
Web: http://www.thomsonrights.com

ISBN: 0-15-507414-8

Wadsworth/Thomson Learning
10 Davis Drive
Belmont, CA 94002-3098
USA

Asia
Thomson Learning
5 Shenton Way #01-01
UIC Building
Singapore 068808

Australia
Nelson Thomson Learning
102 Dodds Street
South Melbourne, Victoria 3205
Australia

Canada
Nelson Thomson Learning
1120 Birchmount Road
Toronto, Ontario M1K 5G4
Canada

Europe/Middle East/Africa
Thomson Learning
High Holborn House
50/51 Bedford Row
London WCIR 4LR
United Kingdom

Latin America
Thomson Learning
Seneca, 53
Colonia Polanco
11560 Mexico D.F.
Mexico

Spain
Paraninfo Thomson Learning
Calle/Magallanes, 25
28015 Madrid, Spain

CONTENTS

PREFACE

Just yesterday, in my course on race and ethnicity in American history, an undergraduate posed the question "Will America ever stop arguing and debating these issues?" I answered unequivocally, "No. Never." She replied, "Why not?" So I launched into a dialogue I have expressed many times over the years, one which I believe in wholeheartedly. "Because we are one of the most ethnically complex societies in the world, and because we also believe in individual equality and individual civil rights." Such complexity, combined with such a high standard, guarantees conflict, and conflict guarantees debate. In fact, that very debate is at the core of our identity. To be American is to debate individual rights. We have never been without the debate, and until we truly achieve individual equality, we will never be without it. A few months ago, my four-year-old granddaughter, Kennedy, who lives in Baton Rouge, Louisiana, asked me, "Boppa, do black people and white people not like each other?" As long as four-year-olds ask such questions, Americans will be debating the meaning of race and ethnicity. I hope that *Equality Deferred* will help illuminate that debate.

A number of people have been very helpful over the years in making *Equality Deferred* a reality, none more so than my wife, Judy, whose own courses on linguistics and multicultural education have generated between us a vigorous series of debates over the years. The librarians at the Newton Gresham Library of Sam Houston State University have been generous with their time and expertise. My colleague, Robert Shadle, has been especially generous with his time in helping me locate information. But, above all others, I must acknowledge the assistance of my students at Sam Houston University, who have forced me to think clearly about race and ethnicity and who have given me hope and confidence that the future is bright, that Americans as a people can do a much better job getting along with one another and fulfilling the promise of the Declaration of Independence.

James S. Olson
Huntsville, Texas

Part

I

THE AGE OF INNOCENCE, 1945–1965

On August 14, 1945, with its economy in ruins, its military destroyed, and atomic bombs threatening nuclear annihilation, Japan surrendered unconditionally. Newspapers and radios carried the story to every home in America, and people thronged the streets, deliriously celebrating a victory that had come at an enormous cost. Neighbors hugged one another on sidewalks, strangers shook hands in jubilation, and millions uttered silent prayers of gratitude. In history's greatest struggle between good and evil, good had triumphed. Adolf Hitler and Benito Mussolini were in their graves, Hideki Tojo was about to go on trial for war crimes, and fascism everywhere was on the run. As many as 100 million people around the world had been killed, victims of German and Japanese arrogance, and most Americans were convinced that without the United States, hundreds of millions of others would be dead as well. In cities and towns throughout the country, Americans thanked democracy, free enterprise, and the hand of God for victory. Fascism's malignant racism had been crushed. An editorialist in the *Houston Post* noted, "Thanks be to God for our deliverance. Freedom, equality, and liberty—the sinews of our great country—will now bind the world for a glorious future."

The soldiers returned to a grateful nation. Small towns and big cities feted the veterans in parades, and Congress passed the GI Bill of Rights to help them attend college and purchase homes. Veterans married their sweethearts and fathered children, producing what would become known as the "baby boom" generation. The economy prospered, and the United States seemed the land of milk and honey. An entire nation held sacred the memory of the more than 250,000 soldiers who had died on distant battlefields.

They also mourned the 25,000 or so servicemen listed as "missing in action," men whose bodies had never been recovered or whose deaths had no eyewitnesses. Throughout Europe and the Pacific, American occupation forces engaged in a systematic attempt to recover the dead. Week after week and month after month in the late 1940s, they searched the battlefields, hunting for weather-tattered uniforms, dog tags, and bones. In the summer of 1948, a squad of sweat-soaked U.S. Army troops, laboring in the muggy heat of the Philippines, picked up a flash of light from the jungle floor. Sunlight had reflected off a metal dog tag, and upon closer examination they found bones and bits of green army fatigues, the remains of Felix Longoria of Three Rivers, Texas. The bones were handed over to army morticians, who certified their identity and placed them in a coffin.

At Subic Bay on the island of Luzon, Longoria's coffin, along with dozens of others, was loaded into the hold of a navy freighter. The men had died as part of General Douglas MacArthur's crusade to wrest the Philippines from Japanese control. The freighter steamed to Guam in the Marianas and from there to Pearl Harbor and San Francisco, where the caskets were shrouded in American flags before being loaded onto Union Pacific and Southern Pacific boxcars. They were headed home for burial, where honor guards would salute them, buglers would play taps, and local newspapers would pay homage to democracy's fallen warriors.

The Southern Pacific train with Longoria's body made its way back to Three Rivers, Texas, by way of Los Angeles, Phoenix, El Paso, and San Antonio. His wife greeted the casket in San Antonio and then had it driven to Three Rivers for burial. Perhaps she expected a hero's welcome. Her husband, the father of her children, had, after all, made the ultimate sacrifice, fighting and dying for freedom and equality on the other side of the world. But the grieving widow was in for a surprise, and so was the rest of America. In 1948, Three Rivers, Texas, had only one mortician and only one funeral home, and its Anglo owner refused to hold services in his chapel for Longoria. "I can't have a dead greaser inside the building," he told a friend. "It'd be bad for business." The wire services picked up the story, and within days it was headlined all over the country. Throughout the United States, Americans denounced the funeral director's stand, and Senator-elect Lyndon B. Johnson intervened, securing a spot in Arlington National Cemetery for Longoria's body.

So much for liberty, equality, and democracy. The Longoria case reminded everyone that Berlin and Tokyo did not have a monopoly on racism, that back home in "the land of the free and the home of the brave," people of color faced a virulent racism that rendered them second-class citizens. Felix Longoria was good enough to die for his country but not good enough to receive a decent burial. "Good God," President Harry Truman uttered when he learned of the controversy. "What are we coming to?"

Chapter One

ETHNIC AMERICA IN 1945

Americans heaved a collective sigh of relief when the war ended in 1945. The previous half-century had exacted a toll on the country's identity. After decades of industrialization, urbanization, and immigration, as well as two world wars and the Great Depression, America's rural, agrarian, isolationist roots seemed all but invisible. Also gone were the bucolic images of America as a nation of White farmers of British, German, and Scandinavian descent working the virgin land of North America. Although the future seemed bright with hope, it was complicated by, in 1945, an American society more diverse than ever. For over 400 years, Americans had been obsessed with their diversity, worrying about how to reconcile the centrifugal forces of race, religion, language, and national origins with the ideals of democracy and equality. Ethnicity had been the marrow of American history, and the postwar years would prove to be no different.

AN ETHNIC GEOGRAPHY

In 1945, the U.S. population was more than 150 million people, most of whom possessed distinct ethnic identities as members of a racial minority or as immigrants or the descendants of immigrants. The African American population exceeded 16 million people. A majority of Blacks still resided in the South, but since the beginning of the Great Migration in 1914, millions had settled in northern and western cities.

Limited educational opportunities and job discrimination confined most Blacks to low-paying jobs, but there had been some progress since the dismal days of Reconstruction. A small elite of educated Black professionals and businessmen existed in every African American community, and during the 1930s the Congress of Industrial Organizations (CIO), a labor union that targeted industrial workers, had actively recruited Black members and treated them equally to Whites.

The Mexican American community had also experienced dramatic change. In 1945, the vast majority of America's 3 million Mexican Americans lived in California, Arizona, New Mexico, Colorado, and Texas. Before the outbreak of the Mexican Revolution of 1911, the Mexican American population had totaled only 400,000 people, but during the next two decades, to escape poverty and revolutionary violence at home, nearly 1.5 million Mexicans headed north. Alejandro Ortiz, an immigrant who reached Los Angeles in 1928, later said of his decision, "I had a family; if I had stayed in Mexico, the kids would have never had a chance of doing better than me."

The Native American population stood at 550,000 in 1945, more than twice its size in 1910. When the first Europeans reached the New World in 1492, the indigenous population of what is today the United States may have been as many as 10 million people, but European diseases, to which Indians had no immunities, soon took a terrible toll. By 1607, when English colonists settled Jamestown, the indigenous inhabitants of what would become the United States totaled approximately 2 million people. That number dropped to 600,000 in 1776, 350,000 in 1870, and only 225,000 in 1910. Between 1910 and 1945, the Native American population had rebounded, although the community was still plagued by poverty, disease, and discrimination. The vast majority of the country's Native Americans still lived on hundreds of government reservations, with large concentrations in Arizona, New Mexico, South Dakota, and Oklahoma. Although non-Indians often considered Native Americans a single ethnic group, Indians themselves knew better. More than 100 tribes still functioned socially and politically in 1945, and most Indians remained conscious of tribal membership and loyal to tribal culture.

When World War II ended, Asian Americans also numbered approximately 550,000 people and resided overwhelmingly in Hawaii, California, Oregon, and Washington. Approximately 200,000 people in the Asian community were of Chinese descent; most of them resided in towns and cities and worked as farmers, ran independent businesses, or were service employees. The vast majority of Chinese Americans were Cantonese speakers and traced their ancestry back to southeastern China. The Filipino American population numbered approximately 125,000 people in 1945. They often worked alongside Mexican Americans in the commercial farms of the Southwest. Finally, in 1945 the Japanese American community numbered approximately 240,000 people and lived primarily in Hawaii and along the Pacific Coast.

For the nation's racial minorities in 1945, the melting pot was a pipe dream. Americans paid lip service to the rhetoric of democracy, liberty, and equality of opportunity—to Horatio Alger's rags-to-riches virtues and to the Statue of Liberty's "give me your huddled masses" promise—but most Whites still nursed a litany of racist assumptions and preferred to keep minorities invisible. The "color line" was more like a brick wall, limiting opportunities for Blacks, Hispanics, Asians, and Indians, and the vast majority of these minorities married endogamously within their own racial group. Coming to terms with the reality of racism would consume much of the country's energies in the second half of the twentieth century.

Among Americans of European descent, the ethnic landscape in 1945 was diverse and complicated. The descendants of the "old immigrants"—the English, Scots, Germans, and Scandinavians who had arrived in America before the 1880s—still remained culturally and politically aware of their origins. Roughly 25 million Americans in 1945 claimed English, German, Welsh, Scottish, and Scottish-Irish ancestry; they were scattered widely throughout the United States and enjoyed jobs as skilled workers, farmers, professionals, and white-collar workers. Another 20 million Americans claimed German heritage, and they too were widely scattered, although the so-called "German triangle" between St. Louis, Milwaukee, and Cincinnati was home to most German Americans. The Irish American community in 1945 was distinct and visible, numbering more than 13 million people, most of whom lived in the large metropolitan areas of the Northeast, the Midwest, and New Orleans and San Francisco. Irish Americans tended to be skilled blue-collar workers or civil servants in state and city governments. More than 6 million Americans of Norwegian, Swedish, Danish, and Finnish descent resided in the upper midwestern states of Minnesota, Iowa, North and South Dakota, Illinois, Michigan, and Wisconsin. Approximately 4 million Americans in 1945 claimed French roots. They lived in New England as the descendants of French Canadian immigrants or in Louisiana as Cajuns, the descendants of the eighteenth-century Acadian migration. Finally, as many as 750,000 Americans, most of whom lived in New York, Wisconsin, and Michigan, were of Dutch heritage.

The forces of assimilation exerted great pressure on parochial, Old World identities. That Anglo Americans were White, English-speaking Protestants—Methodists, Baptists, Presbyterians, and Anglicans—made it easier for other Americans, whose roots were identical, to accept them. British Protestant immigrants readily intermarried with one another and with other White Protestants, and within one generation the ties to the Old World had been all but severed. Second- and third-generation Anglo Americans or Scottish Americans were unlikely to define themselves in such terms. Assimilation was slower for non-English-speaking Protestant immigrants, but as soon as English became the first language of their children and grandchildren, Old World identities fragmented. The Central *Verein,* the German immigrant community's most popular organization, saw its membership dwindle from 125,000 people in 1917 to 39,000 in 1945. Other immigrant organizations, such as the Sons of Norway, experienced similar declines as the first and second immigrant generations died out. Most grandchildren of immigrants simply did not feel the pull of Old World loyalties. As they acclimated to American values, they lost touch with the Old World, and in the process, ethnic theaters, language schools, political organizations, fraternal societies, and lodges lost much of their appeal.

Some groups resisted assimilation. French Canadians, for example, remained French speakers into the third and fourth generations. They tended to concentrate geographically in New England, and a steady stream of new immigrants arriving every week from Quebec continued to infuse immigrant culture. It was also easy for French Canadians to return to Canada for visits, which reinforced traditional loyalties. Also, French Canadian ethnic identity—a curious mix of French culture, Roman Catholicism, and anti-English attitudes—inspired a sense of segregation. Cajun culture in Louisiana was equally resilient. Isolated in the swamps and bayous of southwestern Louisiana, the Cajuns kept to themselves and nursed strong suspicions of outsiders. Irish Americans held tightly to their identity as well, largely because it had become so wrapped up in an anti-English, Roman Catholic mind-set and because they enjoyed political clout in major American cities.

But in 1945, most of the "old immigrants" found themselves being absorbed by the institutions of the larger society. The disappearance of Old World languages, the decline in immigration from Europe, the impact of industrialization and modernization, and the seductive appeal of American popular culture all conspired to dissolve the connections between the Old World and the New. "When I got out of high school," remembered Frederick Asbjornsen, the son of Norwegian immigrants, "my father insisted that I join the Sons of Norway. But I got sick of it. All they did every week was sit around, drink beer, debate the scenic beauties of this fjord or that fjord, and bitch about how arrogant the Swedes were and how stupid the Finlanders were. I quit and never went back."

It was different in 1945 for the "new immigrants" and their children. The Old World was still tangible, its tastes and sounds hovering near the surface of their consciousness. Beginning around 1890, immigration patterns to the United States changed dramatically, with the English, Germans, and Scandinavians declining in numbers and the southern and eastern Europeans surging. Between 1877 and 1945, the number of Jews living in America jumped from around 250,000 to 5 million. At the beginning of that period, most had been German Jews with more liberal religious inclinations, but the new migration brought Yiddish-speaking Orthodox Jews from Russia and Poland. They settled in the Northeast, especially in New York City, where they worked in the needle trades and as professionals, entrepreneurs, civil servants, entertainers, and intellectuals. The Jewish immigrants put a premium on education and, not surprisingly, enjoyed an upward mobility unknown to most other immigrant groups. Finally, in 1945 American Jews got a fuller picture of the Holocaust, and as they learned of the deaths of 6 million of their brothers and sisters in Nazi death camps, their collective identity acquired a sharp political edge.

Italy had also sent millions of immigrants to the United States during the Great Migration. At the end of World War II, the Italian American community exceeded 6 million people, and like the Jewish immigrants, they preferred the cities of the Northeast (especially New York City) and Midwest, with visible concentrations also in New Orleans and San Francisco. Their homeland had been the Mezzogiorno (the six provinces of Abruzzi, Campania, Apulia, Basilicata, Calabria, and Sicily), where most of them had been *contadini,* or peasants, working on large *latifundia* (landed) estates. In the United States, they became a working-class people suspicious of education and non-Italians and highly loyal to their families. At first, they took menial jobs abandoned by upwardly mobile British, Irish, German, and Scandinavians, working in factories, wharves, mines, quarries, mills, smelteries, and sweatshops, but by the end of World War II, large numbers of Italians had found their way into skilled trades and small businesses.

The Great Migration had also brought millions of Slavic immigrants—Poles, Czechs, Slovaks, Rusins, Ukrainians, Croatians, Serbs, Slovenes, Russians, Belorussians, and Bulgarians—to the United States. The Slavic immigrants generally avoided the cities of the Northeast for the urban Midwest, where they took jobs in the mines, mills, factories, and forges of Pennsylvania, upstate New York, Ohio, Indiana, and Illinois. By 1945, such major cities as Chicago, Milwaukee, Cleveland, Pittsburgh, and Buffalo all possessed large Slavic communities. As many as 200,000 Romanian immigrants and their descendants lived in those cities as well.

Finally, Greece had sent hundreds of thousands of immigrants to the United States, and in 1945 their population exceeded 500,000 people. Although some Greeks found work on farms, especially in California, they became primarily an urban people, laboring in factories and running small businesses.

THE ETHNIC CITY

In 1945 the diversity of ethnic America was most visible in major cities, where African Americans, Mexican Americans, European Americans, and Asian Americans clustered together in a cultural cauldron. Racial minorities were often residentially concentrated—African Americans in the rural South and northern ghettoes, the Chinese in San Francisco, Mexican Americans in the Southwest, the Portuguese in Fall River, Massachusetts, and Native Americans on reservations—but among European Americans, massive concentrations of single ethnic groups in tight geographic areas were relatively uncommon. There were some—Jews and Italians in New York City, the Irish in Boston, or the Poles in Chicago—but ethnically mixed neighborhoods were the norm. In the mill towns of New England, for example, Portuguese, Irish, Italians, and French Canadians labored side by side at the looms and lived in the same neighborhoods. So did Slavs, Italians, Lithuanians, Germans, and Czechs in the stockyards of Chicago or Arabs, Poles, and Italians in the automobile plants of Detroit.

In the urban neighborhoods of 1945, ethnic institutions flourished and provided a sense of community. Outsiders often labeled such communities "ghettoes," but they were neither walled, escape-proof fortresses nor pathological expressions of fear and discontent. For many immigrants and their descendants, the urban neighborhoods were havens, not prisons, and eased the adjustment to American life. In the Chinatowns, Polonias, Little Tokyos, and Little Italys of America, immigrants were able to purchase time enough to smooth their transition to the New World. The sights, sounds, and smells of urban ethnic neighborhoods hearkened back to the Old World, reminding the first generation of home and giving the second generation an appreciation for their roots. In Italian neighborhoods, the immigrants enjoyed restaurants selling wine, cheese, salami, hard bread, and pasta. They read newspapers like *L'Italia* in Chicago or *L'Eco d'Italia* in New York. They smelled tomatoes and garlic drying outdoors, heard their own dialects spoken on the street, and attended operas and comedies at theaters catering to Sicilians or Abruzzians or Calabrians. Czech Americans in Chicago joined a local *sokol* society or the Czech-Slavonic Benevolent Society, read the newspaper *Zensky Listy,* and attended the Cyril and Methodius Roman Catholic Parish. In New York City, Jews sat together in cafes on Hester Street, attended Yiddish theaters, and discussed religion and politics. Germans in Cincinnati and St. Louis frequented beer gardens, bowling alleys, shooting galleries, and Lutheran and Catholic churches. And in San Francisco, Chinese immigrants joined *hui kuan* and *tong* immigrant societies and celebrated New Year's and the Festival of the Dead. Ethnic America in 1945 revolved around the churches, coffeehouses, restaurants, shops, gangs, festivals, holidays, societies, and theaters of the urban neighborhoods.

Ethnically mixed urban environments actually sharpened, for a time, the immigrant sense of identity. Living with the so-called stranger next door—a neighbor who spoke a different language, attended a different church, ate different foods, and celebrated different holidays—made immigrants even more aware of their distinctiveness. Theodore White, a Jewish American who grew up in Boston, remembered the mystique of the Catholic church in his neighborhood, the Irish gangs, and the Italian religious festivals: "Almost every hour of every day when I was a kid," he wrote years later, "I knew who I was and who I was not. I was a Jewish kid, not Irish or Italian. Those other people seemed strange to me, and so did their churches, their jokes, their food, and their accents."

The ethnic neighborhoods were demographically as well as culturally dynamic; they were not static places occupied by the same people for generations. The poor, urban immigrants of the twentieth century were just as upwardly mobile as their rural, nineteenth-century predecessors. In the nineteenth-century American cities, the rich often lived downtown, near the seats of political and economic power, whereas the immigrants resided near the warehouses, wharves, and railroad terminals where they worked. But as streetcars, subways, and elevated trains crowded the downtown and linked the city to the outlying suburbs, the rich began relocating, where they could enjoy peace and quiet but still have access to the city center. Poor immigrants or their children filled the vacuum, often converting the former homes of the well-to-do into multifamily tenements. As soon as they could save enough money and afford to move out themselves, the immigrants or their children followed suit, purchasing homes in outlying areas. By the 1890s, for example, many second-generation Irish had left Manhattan in New York City for Queens or even Nassau County, on Long Island, and by the 1920s and 1930s some Italian Americans were doing the same.

So although Greek, Polish, Italian, Jewish, Irish, and other enclaves survived in the cities, they were not usually occupied by the same people, at least not for more than a few years. The immigrant poor were known for their geographic mobility, moving frequently from tenement to tenement, street to street, and neighborhood to neighborhood, and then, once they had acquired the necessary resources, from city to bedroom community or to suburb. More recent immigrants then crowded into the same tenements. Slowly over the course of several generations, the ethnic composition of neighborhoods might change. In New York City, Harlem went from English and German to Irish and Italian and then to African American and Hispanic. Generally between 1890 and 1945, ethnic enclaves had served as way stations from which immigrants and their children moved on to new neighborhoods.

New Identities

Among the ethnic minorities, national identities in 1945 were just as fluid as their neighborhoods, and the forces of assimilation worked steadily to break down parochial loyalties. The pace of assimilation varied from group to group, but the reality of assimilation was undeniable. Geographic mobility, industrialization, the increasing influence of the mass media, the adoption of English, the passage of time, and declining rates of immigration from Europe weakened ties to the Old World. The United States was not a single melting pot but rather a series of melting pots. At the first, the German immigrants of Cincinnati or Milwaukee, for example, grouped themselves according to their origins in the Old World—Prussia, the Palatinate, Bavaria, Württemberg, Swabia, Darmstadt, Schleswig-Holstein, and the Weser valley. For the first generation, those Old World regional identities meant something, but they meant little or nothing to the second generation, who simply considered their ancestry, and themselves, to be German.

The Italian immigrants in New York City at first settled along regional lines as well. On Mott Street between East Houston and Prince were Neopolitans, whereas across the street lived the Basilicati. The Genoese owned Baxter Street and the Sicilians Prince Street. Mott Street between Broome and Grand was Calabrian territory. In Chicago, immigrants from Altavilla in Sicily lived on Larrabee Street, whereas villagers from Aimena, Sicily, and Shiusa Sclafani occupied Cambridge Street. Milton Street held immigrants from Sambuca-Zabut village in Sicily. But as the first Italian generation gave way to the second, Old World village loyalties became irrelevant, and among the third generation even the regional identity lost strength. A third-generation Abruzzian immigrant girl had no difficulty marrying a third-generation Calabrian boy, and they increasingly identified themselves simply as Italian.

Japanese immigrants in San Francisco, known as Issei, grouped themselves according to which of the eleven prefectures in Japan from which they had come; membership in their *kenjinkai* immigrant aid associations reflected prefectural origins as well. But to second-generation Japanese Americans, Nisei, the regional origins of their parents meant little. They readily married other Nisei regardless of the prefectural origins of their parents, and in the process forged a broader identity as Japanese Americans. Similar processes were at work among Syrians, Jews, Romanians, Poles, and Czechs.

By 1945, the forces of assimilation had largely blurred regional identities among the urban ethnic communities, but breakdowns in national ethnic identities occurred as well. Many immigrants began to acquire identities based on occupation. In the needle trades, Jewish, Syrian, and Italian workers suffered poverty and exploitation, and in the process they acquired a class identity nurtured by such labor unions as the Amalgamated Clothing Workers and the International Ladies Garment Workers Union. The United Mine Workers and the United Steel Workers labored to build a similar consciousness among Irish, Italian, and Slavic workers in Ohio, Pennsylvania, Indiana, Illinois, and Michigan. In Detroit, the United Automobile Workers organized Greeks, Italians, Syrians, Poles, Slovaks, Serbs, and Croatians into one union. The unions urged members to learn English, secure U.S. citizenship, and vote—all of which helped immigrant workers to transcend narrow cultural loyalties for broader economic ones. Finally, during the Great Depression, massive unemployment reinforced class loyalties.

So did American politics. Blue-collar immigrant workers—usually Jewish, Eastern Orthodox, or Catholic in religion—regardless of their ethnic background joined labor unions and overwhelmingly voted Democratic. They perceived the Republican Party as the agent of middle- and upper-class Protestants and the business community. During the 1930s and 1940s, organizing the vote and casting a ballot for Franklin D. Roosevelt and Democratic politicians assumed more and more importance in the ethnic communities, and African Americans and Mexican Americans soon followed suit. To many immigrants and their children, being a Democrat was almost as important as being Polish or Italian or Irish.

World War II promoted assimilation as well. During the Civil War, the Spanish American War, and World War I, the military had recruited soldiers along ethnic lines and left them in the same units for the duration. But during World War II, military units were composed of troops from all over the country. Between 1941 and 1945, more than 10 million soldiers were uprooted from their neighborhoods, shipped to military bases across the country and throughout the world, and thrown together in ethnically diverse platoons, companies, and battalions. They trained together, partied together, lived together, fought together, and died together. Sean Brady, a Marine Corps veteran from Hell's Kitchen in New York City, remembered, "Hell, I'd never said a polite word to an Italian in my whole life, and after one week in boot camp, I had a Sicilian as my best friend."

Civilians often had the same experience. Government contracts led to huge increases in industrial production, and factory managers actively recruited workers from rural areas and small towns. The population of major industrial and port cities exploded, and people from diverse ethnic backgrounds found themselves working in the same mills and factories and living in the same housing projects. Cut off from old neighborhoods and extended family ties, they built new relationships that transcended ethnic loyalties and acculturated themselves to new ideas, foods, and phrases.

The fascist threat, the deaths of hundreds of thousands of soldiers, and government propaganda designed to promote national unity inspired an unprecedented outburst of American patriotism. One popular government poster noted, "In a foxhole, there are no Jews or Catholics or Protestants, only freedom-fighting Americans." Schools, civic groups, and the military promoted unity, not diversity. And the fact that millions of immigrants or their children were fighting for Uncle Sam left them feeling more American than ever before.

Finally, the rise of the mass media promoted the English language, American pop culture, and the consumption of standardized products. Radio, mass circulation magazines, and movies undermined foreign language publications and eroded Old World dialects. Between 1920 and 1945, for example, the number of German-language magazines and newspapers in the United States fell from over 300 to seventy. Most third-generation German Americans did not speak or read German and had no reason to subscribe to such publications. During World War II, more than 200 foreign language newspapers ceased publication. Because of radio and film, Americans of all ethnic persuasions appreciated the humor of Jewish comedians like Eddie Cantor and Jack Benny, sports heroes like German American Lou Gehrig, Irish film stars like James Cagney and Bing Crosby, and entertainers like Italian Americans Frank Sinatra and Tony Bennett. Ethnic identities often evaporated in the emerging pop culture of celebrity. In the American melting pot, the demands of national origins and language lost ground first.

For the children of immigrants, the Old World was an abstraction, little more than the nostalgic recollections of homesick parents. They were less likely to track Old World politics, less likely to read Old World news, less likely to dress in Old World clothes, and less likely to adhere to Old World cultural traditions. And by the third generation, when large numbers of the grandchildren of the immigrants could no longer speak or understand the mother tongue, language lost much of its pull on ethnic loyalties. With language and national origins becoming less and less significant, the descendants of the immigrant generation were far more likely to marry outside Old World ethnic groups.

Despite the forces of assimilation, religion still commanded powerful devotions in the ethnic communities, and what had emerged in the United States by 1945 among White ethnics was a triple melting pot—Protestant, Catholic, and Jew—based on religion. In Minnesota, for example, the son of Norwegian immigrants might not marry another Norwegian, but he would still probably marry a Lutheran—Swedish, Danish, or Finnish—or if not a Lutheran then an Episcopalian or a Methodist. As Lutherans, Baptists, Episcopalians, Methodists, and Presbyterians intermarried, a larger White Protestant melting pot emerged. Or in Ohio, the son of a German Catholic might not marry another German but would still marry a Catholic—Irish, Polish, Czech, or Slovak. In fact, a typical German Catholic was more likely to marry a non-German Catholic than a German Protestant. And as Polish, Irish, Italian, Slovak, Czech, French Canadian, and German Catholics intermarried, a White Catholic melting pot appeared in the United States. Finally, a Jewish melting pot developed when German, Polish, and Russian Jews mixed together and married.

OLD REALITIES

Although the forces of assimilation blurred the ethnic identities of the European immigrants and their descendants, America's racial minorities in 1945 remained relatively untouched. To be sure, they had accepted the dynamics of the consumer culture, tuned in to the popular radio programs, watched the most popular films, and purchased, or at least yearned to purchase, fashionable clothes and shiny automobiles. Most of them had bought into the national religion of equality of opportunity, hard work, and economic progress. But their ambitions collided with the reality of White racism. America remained a society where skin color mattered a great deal; many Whites were slow to accept people of color as equals and even slower to extend a hand of friendship and fellowship.

African Americans were especially victimized by the effects of racism. In the South, rigid Jim Crow laws kept Blacks segregated in public and private facilities. Separate schools, universities, bus terminals, restaurants, universities, neighborhoods, waiting rooms, toilets, and drinking fountains stigmatized them and severely limited their economic opportunities. Literacy tests, poll taxes, grandfather

Japanese Americans attending Memorial Day services at the Manzanar, California, War Relocation Authority camp in 1942.

clauses, and White primaries effectively kept Blacks from the polling places and undermined their political power. In the North, even without oppressive Jim Crow statutes on the law books, African Americans found themselves battling the effects of institutional racism. Economic reality and racism limited economic opportunities and confined them to poor, segregated neighborhoods, and because school attendance was based on neighborhood residence, their children often attended large segregated schools. "I left Georgia because I thought Chicago would be different," Willie Jones remembered in 1960. "But up here I still live in a Black neighborhood, shop in Black stores, and watch my children go to Black schools. Things are better here, but not by much."

The Asian communities had challenges of their own. In 1945 approximately 110,000 Japanese Americans, who had spent the war in War Relocation Authority camps, were returning home and trying to rebuild their lives. At every turn, they encountered lingering resentment from many Americans. Daniel Inouye, a Japanese American soldier who lost an arm in combat and went on to become a U.S. senator from Hawaii, remembered getting kicked out of a California barber shop after the war. Chinese Americans had not suffered such indignities during the war, but they knew that being Asian in a European society was a risky and fickle business. Filipinos lived in extreme poverty as migrant workers, trying to subsist picking crops in the Southwest's large commercial farms. They tried to make common cause with Mexican American farm laborers, but cultural differences led to political rivalries, and attempts to politicize both groups failed.

Mexican Americans faced many of the dilemmas encountered by Filipinos and by African Americans. Racism because of their skin color constantly plagued them, limiting opportunities at every level. They made their living in low-paying jobs in factories, railroads, and commercial farms, and faced either Jim Crow segregation laws or institutional racism in many parts of Texas, Oklahoma, New Mexico, Arizona, and California. Poverty, racism, and discrimination plagued them, and they too found voting difficult because of poll taxes, literacy tests, and White primaries. In addition, their children were often forbidden, under threat of punishment, to speak Spanish in public and parochial schools. As a child in California during the 1950s, Richard Rodriguez remembered how much he "missed the sweet rhythms of Spanish and retreated from the harsh, abrupt sounds of English."

Even more uncomfortable in modern American society were Native Americans. Because of different immune systems and poverty, they fell victim to disease and had the shortest life span of any ethnic group in the country. In many western states, including Arizona, New Mexico, and Utah, they were not allowed to vote and therefore could not exercise political power to improve their situations. The assimilationist power of the mass media undermined traditional Native American values, alienated children from parents and grandparents, and cut them adrift in a world that worshiped individualism, competition, technology, and economic change—alien concepts to most Native Americans. Native American novelist N. Scott Momaday remembered seeing a tank from World War II; his description captured the Indian critique of modern technology and how an industrializing society had lost touch with the land:

> Through falling leaves, he saw the machine. It rose up behind the hill, black and massive, looming there in front of the sun. He saw it swell, deepen, and take shape on the skyline, as if it were some upheaval of the earth, the eruption of stone and eclipse, and all about it the glare, the cold perimeter of light, throbbing with leaves. For a moment it seemed apart from the land. . . . Then it came crashing down to the grade, slow as a waterfall, thunderous, surpassing impact, nestling almost into the splash and boil of debris.

During the next several decades, other ethnic groups would express their similar discontents with the nature of American society.

Chapter Two

THE CIVIL RIGHTS CRUSADE

Jackie Robinson was a proud man. Born in southern poverty and raised by a single mother who moved her family to Pasadena, California, he learned early in life the pain of being Black in America; but he managed to transcend it, harnessing his resentments and persevering. A bright, articulate young man, Jackie was also a gifted athlete. He attended Pasadena Junior College and then UCLA, lettering in four varsity sports. He served in the U.S. Army during World War II, and he was commissioned a first lieutenant. Unwilling to quietly accept second-class racial status, his outspoken protests led to a court-martial. He survived the trial, however, and was honorably discharged.

In 1945, Robinson signed on to play baseball with the Kansas City Monarchs of the Negro Leagues. At the time, Branch Rickey, the general manager of the Brooklyn Dodgers, had decided to integrate baseball, and he was looking for a pioneer. He needed a Black athlete who was smart, articulate, talented, and highly disciplined. Dodger scouts told him that Jackie Robinson, shortstop for the Kansas City Monarchs, would probably fill the requirements. After extended discussions with Robinson, Rickey agreed, and he signed Jackie to a contract and sent him to the Montreal Royals, a AAA Dodger farm team. Robinson played second base for the Royals, and in 1947 Rickey brought him up to the majors, starting him at first base for the Dodgers.

Robinson encountered a storm of racist protest, on the field and off, but he faced it all with stoic determination, winning over his enemies with his personal dignity and unparalleled athleticism. Confronted

Photo by U.S.I.A.; Still Pictures Branch, National Archives, NWDNS-306-SSM-4C(54)26

Jackie Robinson and his son attending a 1963 civil rights march in Washington, D.C.

by pitchers who threw at him, players who spiked him, and opposing coaches and White fans who shouted racial insults at him, Robinson took it all and played the game. On the road, he was often denied access to hotels and restaurants, but he kept his peace, letting his bat and glove speak for him and becoming a hero to millions of African Americans. He was named rookie of the year. The Dodgers moved him to second base in 1948. The next year, he won the award as the National League's best-fielding second baseman, and he won the batting title. That year, he was also named the league's most valuable player. When he retired in 1957, Robinson had a lifetime batting average of .311 and a guaranteed spot in baseball's Hall of Fame at Cooperstown.

If the civil rights movement had a hall of fame, Jackie Robinson would occupy the rotunda. His athletic gifts won him a national spotlight, and his intelligence and demeanor garnered the admiration and respect of millions of Whites who decided that there was no place for segregation in sports. It was not much of a jump for many Whites to conclude that racial segregation of any form in American life was immoral. As his wife later wrote, Robinson knew that he was carrying a big weight and that if he failed the entire integration effort would suffer a terrible setback. But he did not fail. He became one of the greatest players of his day, and baseball led American society in the area of integration.

LEGAL BATTLEFIELDS

The end of World War II was an auspicious time for the birth of the civil rights crusade that would dominate American politics during the 1950s and 1960s. Throughout the war years, the U.S. government manufactured a steady stream of antifascist propaganda, and American popular culture reflected a similar point of view. Americans could hardly mention the Axis powers—Germany, Italy, and Japan—without in the same breath raising the specter of dictatorship, genocide, Holocaust, and oppression. Against the backdrop of Adolf Hitler, Benito Mussolini, and Hideki Tojo, the American faith in democracy and individual rights stood out in sharp relief, and Americans made the most of it.

In 1945, African Americans, more than at any time in U.S. history, were poised to take advantage of the democratic rhetoric and challenge the fundamental tenets of Jim Crow segregation. During World War II, more than 1 million Blacks served in the armed forces, half of them in overseas deployments where they generally encountered acceptance from Whites. When they left the military in 1945 and returned home, they were less willing to tolerate racism and discrimination. They had fought for their country and had risked their lives in history's greatest struggle for liberty and equality. Black veterans expected more from their country in 1945 than the continuance of Jim Crow racism. "When I got home to Shreveport, Louisiana," remembered Black army veteran Emil Johnson, "the 'White only' and 'Colored only' signs on drinking fountains stuck in my craw. I just wasn't prepared for the same ole, same ole." Most other Black veterans agreed.

Between 1914 and 1945, millions of African Americans abandoned the rural South for factory jobs in northern cities. Large concentrations of African Americans appeared in Boston, New York, Philadelphia, Buffalo, St. Louis, Cleveland, Chicago, Detroit, and Milwaukee, and a lively, prosperous middle class of Black businessmen and professionals served their needs. During the years of the Great Depression, most Black voters switched allegiances, scuttling loyalties to the Republican Party in favor of Franklin D. Roosevelt, the New Deal, and the Democrats. They became a powerful voting bloc in the Democratic Party, and many party officials were prepared to support

Henry Robinson, ex-slave (circa 1938).

modest civil rights initiatives. In such cities as Chicago, Detroit, New York, Cleveland, and Philadelphia, Black voters often held the balance of power. As they began to demand equality, sympathetic Jews and Catholics, who had themselves been the targets of discrimination, threw them their support. In the presidential election of 1948, President Harry Truman cemented Black loyalties by appointing a federal civil rights commission, backing a federal antilynching bill, proposing a ban on poll taxes, and calling for comprehensive federal civil rights legislation. He also issued an executive order desegregating the armed forces.

The Democratic Party, though, suffered from a debilitating schizophrenia. Its strongest, most loyal constituencies became northern Blacks and southern Whites, and the vast divide between the two would shape American politics throughout the twentieth century. The schism was first exposed at the Democratic National Convention of 1948, where President Truman's civil rights initiatives enraged White southerners. Governor Strom Thurmond of South Carolina engineered a Dixiecrat rebellion, and many southern delegates walked out of the convention. Thurmond established the States Rights Party and ran for president on its ticket. Defying the odds, Truman won the election, and his victory underscored the new political power of African Americans. They would use that influence to promote a civil rights agenda.

The federal courts became the first battle line drawn in the civil rights wars, and the National Association for the Advancement of Colored People (NAACP) was at the forefront of the onslaught. Ever since its formation in 1910, the NAACP had filed lawsuit after lawsuit in state and federal courts, taking aim at the most egregious examples of *de jure* (by law) discrimination, but most of their battles had been fought in vain. Not until the case of the Scottsboro boys in the 1930s did the NAACP achieve a stunning victory that drew national attention.

In March 1931, nine young Black men hitched a ride on a train in Alabama, hoping to find work in another town. During the trip they got into a fight with a group of White youths. The young White men, after being ejected from the train, complained to the local sheriff, and at the next stop, deputies arrested the nine Blacks and two White women traveling with them. The women, perhaps worried about being prosecuted for prostitution, claimed to have been gang raped, and the deputies then hustled the accused rapists to the county seat in Scottsboro. Thus began the saga of the "Scottsboro boys."

They went on trial in April. Although the Sixth Amendment guarantees legal representation to indigent criminal defendants, the Scottsboro defendants received scandalously inadequate counsel. The trial judge allowed them only a brief, twenty-minute discussion with attorneys before the trial, and he systematically excluded Blacks from the jury, denying the defendants another of their Sixth Amendment rights. Although the two women's stories were riddled with inconsistencies and physicians found no physical evidence of rape, the first two defendants were convicted in a one-day trial. Outside the courtroom, when the verdict was announced, 10,000 spectators cheered wildly, and a brass band began playing marching music. During the next three weeks all the defendants were convicted except the 13-year-old; the judge declared a mistrial in his case. The eight others were sentenced to death.

The case—*Powell v. Alabama*—became a cause célèbre for civil rights advocates. Attorneys for the NAACP worked up an appeal, and *Powell v. Alabama* went to a higher court. The Alabama Supreme Court upheld seven of the convictions while reversing the conviction of the youngest defendant. The case then entered the federal courts, and on November 7, 1932, by a vote of seven to two, the U.S. Supreme Court reversed all of the convictions on the grounds that the defendants, by not having access to legal counsel, had been denied their Fourteenth Amendment right to due process.

The national controversy over the Scottsboro case ricocheted through the federal court system. On April 1, 1935, the Supreme Court decided the fate of Clarence Norris, one of the Scottsboro defendants who had been retried, reconvicted, and sentenced again to death. Norris's NAACP attorneys argued that because Alabama had excluded African Americans from the trial jury and from the grand jury that had returned the indictment, he had not received a fair trial as dictated by the Fifth, Sixth, and Fourteenth Amendments to the Constitution. By a unanimous vote, the court overturned the conviction, agreeing that Norris had been denied due process. During the next several years, the Scottsboro defendants were tried again and again. By 1937, under intense political pressure and international scrutiny, the state of Alabama dropped charges against five of the young men. Several others were paroled from prison between 1937 and 1940.

Victory in the Scottsboro case energized NAACP attorneys, and during the late 1930s and 1940s they filed dozens of anti-Jim Crow lawsuits. In 1896, the Supreme Court's notorious decision in *Plessy v. Ferguson* had legitimized segregation, upholding "separate but equal" public facilities, and the NAACP was determined to dismantle the decision. Thurgood Marshall, an African American attorney and head of the NAACP's Legal Defense Fund, later recalled, "I made it my life's goal to destroy *Plessy v. Ferguson* because it had destroyed so many of my people's dreams."

Destroy it he did. A 1938 decision heralded the future of Jim Crow. The state of Missouri had denied an African American young man admission to its law school solely on the basis of race, and he sued. The case of *Missouri rel. Gaines v. Canada* made its way through the state and federal courts, with lawyers for the state consistently winning. But the Supreme Court saw things differently. By refusing to admit a Black student to the state law school, the justices decided, Missouri had violated the equal protection clause of the Fourteenth Amendment to the Constitution. Like other Missourians, Blacks paid state taxes and were therefore equally entitled to all state services. By closing off the law school to all Blacks, the state had engaged in racial discrimination.

In 1941, when Harlan Stone became chief justice of the U.S. Supreme Court, NAACP attorneys quickly concluded that he would be sympathetic to their concerns. "Stone understands our position," Marshall confided to colleagues, "and he understands the Constitution. He can be trusted." They were right. During Stone's tenure on the court (1941–1946), the entire edifice of Jim Crow began to crumble, beginning with the *Mitchell v. United States* (1941) case. Railroads moving through the South frequently denied Black passengers access to Pullman cars, where they could sleep on an overnight journey, because White passengers did not want to use the same bed an African American had once occupied. But the Supreme Court agreed with the NAACP's argument that railroads were a form of interstate commerce and that denying Pullman berths on the basis of race violated the Interstate Commerce Act. Five years later, in *Morgan v. Virginia* (1946), the court overturned Virginia statutes requiring segregated seating in buses, particularly if the bus had crossed a state line.

The NAACP also targeted a phalanx of southern statutes designed to keep Blacks from voting. Thurgood Marshall regularly put 50,000 miles a year on his car, driving from city to city and county courthouse to county courthouse throughout the South, filing briefs and arguing cases. In 1941, he scored a major victory in the *Smith v. Allwright* case. Back in the 1890s and early 1900s, most southern states had established the White primary election. Because the South was so solidly Democratic, primary elections, in which candidates were selected, were tantamount to general elections, because Republicans did not stand a chance of winning. To exclude Blacks from voting in the Democratic primary, southern legislatures declared the primary a "private," not "public" institution, because a political party was not the creation of the state. Private groups could discriminate on the basis of race, so the logic went, without violating the Fourteenth and Fifteenth Amendments to the Constitution. Marshall and the NAACP disagreed, arguing that the primary election, because it did select candidates for public office, was at least a quasi-public function and that the White primary robbed Black people of their right to vote. The Supreme Court agreed with Marshall's logic and declared that all-White primaries violated the Fifteenth Amendment.

Harlan Stone died in 1946 and was replaced by Fred Vinson, but the NAACP soon found Vinson to be just as sympathetic, and the legal assault on Jim Crow continued. Two cases in 1948—*Shelley v. Kraemer* and *Hard v. Hodge*—overturned restrictive covenants in public housing projects. The restrictive covenant was a private arrangement among managers of public housing projects not to rent apartments to Black people. But because African Americans were taxpayers whose money supported such government projects, the court ordered, restrictive covenants violated their Fourteenth Amendment rights. The 1949 Supreme Court decision in *Schnell v. Davis* outlawed literacy tests, a device commonly used in the South to disqualify Black voters.

Finally, the Vinson court took the logic of the *Missouri rel. Gaines v. Canada* case and applied it throughout the country. In the wake of *Missouri rel. Gaines,* the state of Texas, hoping to sidestep the argument that denying Blacks a legal education on the basis of race was unconstitutional, had established a separate law school for Blacks. Thurgood Marshall considered such logic repugnant, and he sued. Some of his associates wanted him to argue that the new Texas law school violated *Plessy v. Ferguson*'s "separate but equal" criteria because it had inferior facilities, an inferior law library, and an inferior faculty. But Marshall would have none of it. He considered *Plessy* to be immoral, and he did not want to give it any more legitimacy. Instead, he argued that "separate facilities, equal or unequal, are unconstitutional because they stigmatize Negroes, making them feel inferior." In *Sweatt v. Painter* (1950), the Supreme Court ruled that a separate law school for African Americans was inherently unconstitutional. A few days later, in *McLaughlin v. Oklahoma Board of Regents,* the justices overturned University of Oklahoma regulations that forced an African American graduate student to sit at a separate desk and table. *Sweatt* and *McLaughlin* emboldened Thurgood Marshall and the NAACP. "We have established the legal foundation," he told friends. "Segregation on the basis of race is unconstitutional in higher education. Now we can go after the public schools."

Marshall's crusade culminated in 1954, when the Supreme Court heard a series of five cases dealing with the legality of forced racial segregation in public schools. Lower courts had rejected all the lawsuits, but the NAACP had appealed all five. The outcome was uncertain. Chief Justice Fred Vinson had died in 1953, and Republican President Dwight D. Eisenhower replaced him with Earl Warren, former governor of California. Warren's position on civil rights was a mystery, although the enthusiasm with which he had supported the internment of Japanese Americans during World War II did not bode well.

Marshall argued all five of the cases before the Warren court. The case of *Brown v. Board of Education of Topeka, Kansas* was the first on the docket. It involved Linda Brown, an 11-year-old girl who had to cross a railroad yard to attend a segregated school for Blacks, even though another public school was located across the street. Her father filed the lawsuit, claiming that such school rules and the laws behind them were inherently discriminatory and violations of the Fifth and Fourteenth Amendments to the U.S. Constitution. Marshall put the father's logic before the court. He called on the court to overturn the *Plessy v. Ferguson* doctrine of "separate but equal" on two grounds. First, the supplies and buildings provided to Black students were almost always inferior to those offered to White students. Second, public school segregation ostracized Black children and stigmatized them for being Black, which deprived them of self-esteem and often made them ashamed of their heritage.

Chief Justice Earl Warren was about to reveal his true colors. He agreed with Marshall's contentions but also knew that desegregation would be a bitter pill for the South to swallow. Only a unanimous decision of the Supreme Court, Warren believed, would provide the moral authority needed to overcome centuries of tradition. Behind the scenes, he was indefatigable in securing the full support of the other justices. In a unanimous decision, the court decided that "separate but equal" public accommodations and schools were inherently unequal. *Plessy v. Ferguson* was dead, and the Fourteenth Amendment to the Constitution had been restored. Marshall was ecstatic. "Can you believe it," he told his staff. "A unanimous decision. It's all I could have ever hoped for."

Marshall would soon learn that dreams are sometimes very difficult to fulfill. The Supreme Court had ruled, but the willingness of White southerners to obey was quite a different matter. Governor Herman Talmadge of Georgia called the *Brown* decision "a mere scrap of paper." In many ways he was right. White southerners and their politicians at the federal, state, and local levels organized what became known as massive resistance to the court-ordered desegregation. At first, southern state legislatures passed "interposition" statutes nullifying federal court orders in individual states, but the Civil War had long since decided that issue, declaring the federal government sovereign and forcing the states to obey the laws of Congress and the decisions of the federal courts. The Warren court quickly disposed of the interposition statutes.

When that failed, the South tried other legal chicaneries. Local school boards gerrymandered boundaries of school districts to guarantee that most White children and most Black children attended segregated schools. Sometimes the lines drawn were incredibly arcane. In 1957, when Thurgood Marshall looked at a map of the Charleston, South Carolina, school boundaries, he remarked, "The diagram looks more like a can of earthworms than a map." The NAACP filed lawsuits against such racially motivated gerrymandering, and the federal courts ruled unconstitutional all such arrangements whose sole purpose was to maintain segregated public schools. When gerrymandering failed, many southern legislatures tried to provide public funds to pay the tuition of White children attending segregated private schools. The Supreme Court soon terminated that practice. As a last resort, southern state legislatures tried to cut funding to all integrated public schools. That too failed, but the dodging and delaying had worked. As late as 1960, six years after the *Brown* decision, only 1 percent of southern schools had integrated.

MARTIN LUTHER KING, JR., AND CIVIL DISOBEDIENCE

Southern intransigence in response to the *Brown* decision convinced many people in the civil rights community that they could not depend on the law to redeem the promises of the U.S. Constitution. For all of its work and all of its victories over the previous four decades, the NAACP still had not managed to desegregate the schools, even with the backing of the U.S. Supreme Court. Black people were still consistently denied the right to vote. Only more direct, confrontational tactics, many concluded, could convince White segregationists to back down.

The first showdown occurred in 1955 in Montgomery, Alabama. Local ordinances there required Black people to sit in the backs of buses. No African American was allowed to sit in the same row of seats or in any row to the front of White riders. In fact, no Blacks under any circumstances could sit in the front rows of a bus, and they had to give up their seats in middle rows and move back if Whites needed the seats. The local branch of the NAACP decided to test the ordinance legally. On December 1, 1955, Rosa Parks, a 43-year-old Black seamstress, refused to give up her seat to a White rider. Even though the bus driver tried to get her to move back, she refused and was arrested. She was fined $10.

The NAACP then went into action. Black people constituted 75 percent of the city's bus riders, and the NAACP organized a boycott. Blacks stopped riding the buses. NAACP leaders promised to continue the boycott until Black riders were treated with courtesy, and more Black bus drivers were hired. They did not even demand repeal of the ordinance requiring Blacks to sit in the back of the bus; they only demanded that once on the bus, a Black rider would not have to give his or her seat to a White rider. All but a few of Montgomery's 48,000 Black residents joined the boycott.

The boycott produced immediate results. Several NAACP leaders had their houses firebombed, Blacks walking to work were beaten, and White supremacists fired handguns and rifles at Black riders. Alabama public officials, enraged at what one state legislator described as "nigger NAACP insolence," demanded that the state office for the National Association for the Advancement of Colored People hand over its membership lists. Ostensibly, the police were going to search for "radicals and Communists." But the NAACP refused to comply and appealed to the U.S. Supreme Court. In 1958, the Supreme Court rendered its decision in *NAACP v. Alabama,* upholding the NAACP's refusal to hand over its membership lists to state police.

The boycott also produced one of the greatest leaders in American history—the Rev. Martin Luther King, Jr. He was a 26-year-old minister with a doctorate in theology who preached at the Dexter Avenue Baptist Church in Montgomery. Bright, charismatic, passionate, and courageous, King managed to sustain the boycott, despite its dangers and inconveniences, telling his followers, "There comes a time when people get tired. We are here . . . to say to those who have mistreated us so long that we are tired—tired of being segregated and humiliated, tired of being kicked about by the brutal feet of oppression. . . . We have come here tonight to be saved from the patience that makes us patient with anything less than freedom and justice."

King did not advocate violence, only firm, nonviolent protest. For 381 days the vast majority of African Americans in Montgomery remained steadfast, refusing to ride the Jim Crow buses. They carpooled, hitchhiked, rode bikes, and walked, but they stayed off the buses. The boycott was an effective economic tool, and it dramatized King's message to the rest of America. It was also successful, indicating to others that similar nonviolent, economic pressure would have positive results. The city fathers of Montgomery, as the boycott brought the city's transportation to the brink of financial ruin, caved in and repealed the segregation ordinance. In the meantime, the NAACP took the segregation ordinance to court, and in 1956 the Supreme Court ended the boycott by declaring racial segregation in public transportation facilities unconstitutional.

The vortex of the civil rights movement then shifted from Montgomery, Alabama, to Little Rock, Arkansas, where federal courts had ordered the desegregation of the city's public schools. Nine Black students registered to attend Central High School. On September 2, 1957, the day before school began, Governor Orval Faubus announced that he would not extend police protection to Black children. The Black students, dubbed the Little Rock Nine by journalists, showed up for school on September 4, 1957, but the Arkansas National Guard surrounded Central High and would not let them enter.

President Dwight D. Eisenhower, trying to avoid a constitutional crisis, met with Governor Faubus and convinced him to remove the National Guard troops. But on September 23, when the nine Black students tried to attend school, an angry mob gathered outside the school and threatened them. When the mob refused to disperse the next day, Eisenhower nationalized the Arkansas National Guard, which put them under his command, and deployed regular army troops from the 101st Airborne Division to protect the Black students. The Little Rock Nine began their first day of school on September 25. But, Faubus was not finished. Masses of White students left Central High, effectively closing down the school in 1958 and 1959. Faubus tried to start a system of private schools for White students, but the movement petered out. In 1959, Central High School opened as an integrated high school. "When I looked at the faces of those boys and girls," Jackie Robinson later recalled, "I was so proud of them and so ashamed of my country. Nothing I went through matched the terror they faced and the courage with which they faced it."

The events of 1957 pushed President Eisenhower toward federal civil rights legislation. To most Americans, the southern position was untenable. The Supreme Court had ordered desegregation of the public schools, and southern opposition seemed to undermine the rule of law. And the televised images of Black children trying to go to school and being confronted by screaming, racist Whites further convinced most Americans that some type of federal legislation was necessary. In

1957, Congress passed and President Eisenhower signed the Civil Rights Act, which established a civil rights division in the justice department and created a federal civil rights commission to investigate reports of discrimination on the basis of race, religion, color, or national origins. The legislation also prohibited discrimination in voting rights. Ironically, the civil rights commission had no power to act on its investigations or to punish violators. Congress remedied that with the Civil Rights Act of 1960, which gave the civil rights commission enforcement teeth and made it a federal offense to obstruct civil rights orders issued by federal courts.

"Nothing is so powerful as an idea whose time has come," French novelist Victor Hugo wrote in the nineteenth century, and equality's time had arrived in the United States. The highest court in the land had condemned segregation as a violation of Fourteenth Amendment rights, and Martin Luther King's boycott of the buses of Montgomery, Alabama, had demonstrated the power of direct action. Other Americans joined King in assuming the mantle of civil disobedience and direct action, and the country would never be the same.

In January 1957, just after city officials in Montgomery, Alabama, had agreed to desegregate the city's buses, Black ministers from ten southern states met at the Ebenezer Baptist Church in Atlanta to establish the Southern Christian Leadership Conference (SCLC), and they elected King to head the organization. The SCLC committed itself to desegregation of public schools, public transportation, and public facilities and to the right of Black people to vote. The ministers followed King's lead, urging Blacks to refuse to cooperate with the institutions of a segregated society and to engage in nonviolent civil disobedience and mass protest.

The first African Americans to act on the recommendations of King and the SCLC were students at the Negro Agricultural and Technical College in Greensboro, North Carolina. On February 1, 1960, four students entered a Woolworth's department store, sat down at the lunch counter, and ordered coffee. When the manager denied them service because they were Black, they refused to leave the store, sitting there until closing time. One of the students was Jesse Jackson. The next day, eighty-five North Carolina A&T students crowded into Woolworth's, disrupting business and driving away White customers. The press dubbed their demonstration a "sit-in." Civil rights activists soon exported the tactic throughout the South, conducting sit-ins at stores, doctors' offices, movie theaters, bus and train stations, and restaurants.

Inspired by the sit-ins, a group of sixteen White and Black students in Raleigh, North Carolina, established the Student Nonviolent Coordinating Committee (SNCC). Its leaders were Robert Moses and James Forman. SNCC's goal was to desegregate America and register

Black voters in the South. SNCC recruited college students from around the country and set up field offices throughout the South. Employing the tactics of nonviolent civil disobedience, they intentionally violated segregation statutes by using drinking fountains and rest rooms labeled "White only" and sitting down in "White only" sections of movie theaters, restaurants, public parks, and beaches. SNCC voter registration teams went into Mississippi to sign up Blacks to vote. They were arrested by the hundreds, which only played into SNCC hands. "They can't arrest us all," Forman proclaimed. "There won't be enough room in all the jails of the South to hold us."

In 1961, the Congress of Racial Equality (CORE) decided to test whether Supreme Court orders to desegregate interstate public transportation in the South were being obeyed. In 1960, its *Boynton v. Virginia* decision had expanded on the *Morgan v. Virginia* decision and concluded that a bus terminal operated as an "integral" part of interstate bus service and could not segregate passengers who were on a trip across state lines. CORE selected thirteen young people—seven Blacks and six Whites—to board a bus in Washington, DC, and travel through the South to New Orleans. Along the way they were to peacefully resist attempts to segregate them. CORE widely publicized the "freedom rides," and the national media picked up on the story. In Anniston, Virginia, White mobs stoned and firebombed one bus, and in Birmingham, Alabama, a mob of White racists stopped a bus, pulled out the freedom riders, and savagely beat them, all in sight of newspaper photographers and television news cameras. "My God," exclaimed Attorney General Robert Kennedy, "I don't think I've ever seen such hatred in my life. It's extraordinary." The Southern Christian Leadership Conference and the Student Nonviolent Coordinating Committee then dispatched thousands of freedom riders into the South, overwhelming local authorities and making it impossible to enforce segregationist statutes. CORE had achieved exactly what it had set out to do—focus national attention on southern racism and Jim Crow statutes.

Civil rights activists were also concerned about the snail's pace of school desegregation. In 1961, despite the Supreme Court's 1954 *Brown* decision, less than 30 percent of southern school districts had desegregated. Higher education was not much better. In 1962, Governor Ross Barnett of Mississippi defied a court order and refused to enroll James Meredith at the University of Mississippi in Oxford. He used every weapon in his racist arsenal to keep the young Black man out. President Kennedy found Barnett's behavior so frustrating that in the middle of the Cuban missile crisis, he sarcastically joked to his brother, Attorney General Robert Kennedy, "Do you think one of those Russian missiles could reach Oxford and end that mess?" Eventually, Kennedy had to federalize the National Guard to keep order, but not before two people had been killed in the rioting. Meredith enrolled at Ole Miss and later graduated.

In 1963, Governor George Wallace staged an even more dramatic protest to keep Black students out of the University of Alabama. In an act of shameless political posturing, he personally blocked the entrance to the registrar's office. Wallace backed down only when Nicholas Katzenbach, attorney general of the United States, backed by federal marshals and federal troops, ordered him, under threat of arrest, to open the door. An incredulous JFK said, "What a two-bit, pint-sized ass!" In a subsequent speech, the president said, "Surely, in 1963, one hundred years after emancipation, it should not be necessary for an American citizen to demonstrate in the streets for an opportunity to stop at a hotel, or eat at a lunch counter . . . on the same terms as any other American."

Martin Luther King's nonviolent disobedience contrasted sharply with the malignant racism of many southerners, and he used television as a political weapon, knowing that when most Americans witnessed violence against Black people, they would instinctively rally to his cause. That reality became abundantly clear early in 1963, when he organized a series of demonstrations in Birmingham, Alabama, to celebrate the centennial of the Emancipation Proclamation. Demanding desegregation of public facilities and fair employment opportunities, King and thousands of supporters marched through the city's streets. In front of a national television audience, local White police employed high-pressure fire hoses and attack dogs on the protestors. Amid it all, King held the line, turning the other cheek and maintaining his nonviolent vigil.

Southern opponents of the civil rights movement, however, did not restrain themselves. In June 1963, Medgar Evers, director of the Mississippi office of the NAACP, was assassinated by a sniper outside his own home. Civil rights demonstrations then erupted throughout the South, and Martin Luther King's movement accelerated.

On August 28, 1963, King gave the civil rights movement maximum exposure when he assembled more than 250,000 people in Washington, DC. Represented in the throng were the National Association for the Advancement of Colored People, the Southern Christian Leadership Congress, the Student Nonviolent Coordinating Committee, the American Jewish Congress, the National Council of Churches, the American Friends Service Committee, and the American Federation of Labor-Congress of Industrial Organizations (AFL-CIO). They marched from the Washington Monument to the Lincoln Memorial, gathered around the reflecting pool, and listened to several speakers—none of them more eloquent than Martin Luther King whose "I Have a Dream" speech became a moral emblem to America. The crowd sang "We

Photo by U.S.I.A.; Still Pictures Branch, National Archives, NWDNS-306-SSM-4D(89)9

Washington Mall during the massive 1963 civil rights demonstration.

Shall Overcome," the civil rights movement's anthem, and prayed for a new day. After the mass demonstration, President Kennedy held a reception for the march's leaders, including King, Whitney Young of the National Urban League, Roy Wilkins of the NAACP, and Walter Reuther and A. Philip Randolph of the AFL-CIO. In the White House, President Kennedy later told his brother, "You know, this isn't going to go away. It's taken on a life of its own."

Public support for the civil rights movement increased on September 15, 1963, when racists bombed the Sixteenth Street Baptist Church in Birmingham, killing four Black girls in a Sunday school class. The bombing was a seminal event in the civil rights movement. "We face a moral crisis as a people," President Kennedy remarked. "It cannot be met by repressive police action. It cannot be left to increased demonstrations in the streets. It cannot be quieted by token moves or talk. It is a time to act in the Congress, in your state and

Photo by National Park Service; John Fitzgerald Kennedy Library, NLK-WHP-AR-AR7993B-2TT

Martin Luther King, Jr., Robert F. Kennedy, Roy Wilkins, Lyndon Johnson,
Walther Reuther, and others after a 1963 White House meeting on civil rights.

local legislative body and, above all, in all of our daily lives." He then submitted a federal civil rights bill to Congress, which called for integration of all public facilities, even those privately owned, and for the withholding of federal money from segregated institutions.

Kennedy did not live long enough to see the bill become law, but President Lyndon Johnson did. A politician with a southern constituency and a southern twang, Johnson had long soft-peddled his civil rights views, but he had converted to the notion in 1955. While driving in a Cadillac with his wife, two daughters, and their Black maid, from Washington, DC, to Texas, he had stopped in Mississippi to gas up and get some snacks. The store owner would not allow the maid to use the restroom, and she had to walk into the woods to relieve herself. Johnson later remarked, "Here I was, the majority leader of the United States Senate, one of the most powerful men in the country, and one of my female employees had to squat in the bushes to pee. It was not right. It just took me a few more years to do anything about it."

The summer of 1964, known as Freedom Summer in civil rights annals, gave President Johnson the momentum he needed to secure passage of the civil rights bill. The Student Nonviolent Coordinating Committee trained 900 civil rights workers in Ohio, most of them liberal White college students from the North, and sent them to Mississippi in the summer of 1964 to register Black voters. Nine of the White workers were murdered. The most infamous killings took the lives of Michael Schwerner, Andrew Goodman, and James Chaney, who were murdered by Ku Klux Klansmen. Southern racists may have hailed the killings, but to most people, murdering young people who were helping others register to vote seemed un-American. Whatever local notoriety the murderers might have gained, they only fueled the engine of the civil rights movement and guaranteed passage of federal civil rights legislation.

In 1965, civil rights activists switched the focus of their voter registration drives from Mississippi to Alabama. Alabama Whites reacted with all of the frustration and fear of their Mississippi counterparts. The center of the voter registration campaign was Selma, a former entrepôt in the slave trade. Early in 1965, hundreds of civil rights workers associated with the Student Nonviolent Coordinating Committee descended on central Alabama. Sheriff Jim Clark of Selma and his deputies attacked the demonstrators in what rapidly escalated into a police riot. Blacks attempting to register to vote were beaten by club-toting police and attacked by police dogs. Two civil rights activists were beaten to death.

The murders brought Martin Luther King and the Southern Christian Leadership Conference into the battle. A week after the killings, King staged a protest march from Selma to the state capitol in Montgomery. He did not personally attend. The marchers were barely out of town when Alabama state troopers attacked them with tear gas and clubs, all of which was broadcast over national television. As the demonstrators fled back toward town, they were attacked and gassed by Sheriff Clark's deputies. The protestors dispersed.

On March 21, 1965, however, the march commenced again, this time with King among the demonstrators. President Lyndon B. Johnson had federalized 3,000 members of the Alabama National Guard and stationed them all along the highway from Selma to Montgomery. Thousands of liberal Whites and Blacks from the North joined the marchers, and they made their way safely to the state capitol, where King delivered another of his moving speeches for equality and justice. That same night, however, civil rights worker Viola Liuzzo was murdered by Klansmen. Her death convinced President Johnson to move ahead vigorously with the federal civil rights law. He promoted it as a moral good and asked Americans to support it in the name of John F. Kennedy, their fallen president.

In June 1964, Johnson managed to push the U.S. Senate to approve cloture and stop an anti-civil rights filibuster by southern Democrats. The Civil Rights Act of 1964 then quickly became law. It outlawed discrimination in voting, education, and public accommodations;

established the Equal Employment Opportunity Commission to investigate job discrimination; permitted the federal government to freeze funds to state and local agencies not complying with the law; and provided funds to the Department of Health, Education, and Welfare to speed desegregation of the nation's public schools. Opponents immediately sued, focusing on the law's provision that private businesses who served the general public could not discriminate on the basis of race. They claimed that the Civil Rights Act of 1964 was unconstitutional—a violation of an individual's Fifth Amendment right to private property. The case—*Heart of Atlanta Motel, Inc. v. United States*—reached the Supreme Court late in 1964, and the justices upheld the public accommodations section of the Civil Rights Act, asserting that the Fifth Amendment's guarantee of liberty to every American superceded its protection of private property.

But Johnson's civil rights agenda included one more item—protecting the right of African Americans to vote. Decades of White primaries, poll taxes, literacy tests, and outright intimidation had kept them from the voting booths, and Johnson was determined to turn the tide. He enjoyed the support of most Americans, White and Black, who believed that U.S. citizenship conferred the right to vote regardless of race. In 1964, the Twenty-Fourth Amendment to the Constitution was ratified, which outlawed use of poll taxes, in primary and general elections, to keep people from voting. In 1965, Congress passed a second civil rights bill, known as the Civil Rights Act or the Voting Rights Act. By assigning federal marshals to monitor southern elections, the law protected the right of African Americans to vote and limited the effects of violence and intimidation.

By 1965, on the law books at least, the edifice of Jim Crow segregation and *de jure* discrimination had been dismantled. The series of monumental Supreme Court decisions had combined with the civil rights acts of 1957, 1960, 1964, and 1965 to outlaw all forms of racial discrimination. But resistance to the law ran deep in the South. A decade after the *Brown* decision, the Supreme Court found itself still dealing with massive resistance. One such instance was *Griffin v. County School Board of Prince Edward County,* decided by a seven to two vote on May 25, 1964. To prevent desegregation, school officials in Prince Edward County, Virginia, had ordered the closing of all public schools. The court ruled that such a decision was a violation of the equal protection clause of the Fourteenth Amendment. "We have come so far," Martin Luther King told SCLC supporters in 1965, "but we have so far to go. The road to the promised land of freedom and equality is such a long one."

Chapter Three

WELCOMING REFUGEES AND
ENDING QUOTAS, 1945–1965

The euphoria of victory sweeping across the United States in 1945 proved maddeningly ephemeral. All too quickly, World War II gave way to the Cold War, and the bogeyman of Joseph Stalin chased Hitler and Mussolini and Tojo from the pantheon of American fear. For the next twenty years, the Cold War would shape American politics, including debates over immigration, ethnicity, and civil rights.

On July 18, 1949, the impact of the Cold War on American ethnicity became abundantly clear when Jackie Robinson testified before the House Un-American Activities Committee (HUAC). Robinson was called before HUAC to discredit the previous testimony of Paul Robeson, a renowned African American athlete, singer, Communist, and civil rights activist. Back in April, Robeson had suggested in a news conference in Paris that Black men in the United States would never take up arms against the Soviet Union, where people of all races enjoyed "full dignity." The committee wanted to see if Jackie Robinson agreed. Did Paul Robeson represent most Black people, or was he just another Communist guilty of hyperbole? Addressing the committee in his pinched, high-pitched voice, Robinson observed, "Paul Robeson's statement in Paris to the effect that American Negroes would refuse to fight in any way against Russia . . . sounds very silly to me. . . I've got too much invested for my wife and child and myself in the future of this country . . . to throw it away because of a siren song sung in bass."

Such was Cold War politics—two of the country's most influential Blacks pitted against each other. Born in 1898, Robeson grew up in an

America that considered Blacks mentally and athletically inferior to Whites and barred them from most athletic and professional avenues. At home, however, Robeson's parents instilled in him a sense of pride and taught him to prove White America wrong. He graduated from high school as the class valedictorian and tested number one on statewide academic examinations. At Rutger's College, Robeson excelled in debating, sports, singing, and acting. "Equality might be denied," he later wrote, "but I *knew* that I was not inferior." He was an all-American football player, earned varsity letters in three other sports, and was inducted into Phi Beta Kappa, the distinguished academic fraternity.

After graduation, Robeson played professional football, took a law degree at Columbia University, and became a Shakespearean actor and singer. But despite those accomplishments, Robeson never felt fully accepted in American society. Traveling the world, comparing other societies to his own, he was eventually impressed with the Soviet Union, where, he wrote, "I, the son of a slave, walk this earth with complete dignity." Later he told HUAC investigators, "I would say in Russia I felt for the first time a full human being, and no colored prejudice like in Mississippi, and no colored prejudice like in Washington, and it was the first time I felt like a human being, where I did not feel the pressure of color as I feel in this committee today."

Twenty-one years younger than Robeson, Jackie Robinson had a different view of America. To be sure, he too had known the bitter taste of racism. His mother had left Georgia for California to give her children more opportunities, and Robinson had taken advantage of the move. He became a star athlete at UCLA, fought against racism during World War II, and played professional baseball in the Negro Leagues. Then outside social forces swung in his favor. Organized professional baseball—that is, White professional baseball—made the decision to integrate, and Robinson became the man to do it. And he performed, and endured, with grace, determination, and an iron will. But during the Cold War, just being a symbol of America's lofty ideals was not enough. When Robeson spoke out in favor of the Soviet Union, Robinson was called upon to respond. And he did—both opposing Robeson's specific comment while affirming Robeson's general criticism of American society. Black loyalty to America did not mean, Robinson said, that "we're going to stop fighting race discrimination in this country until we've got it licked. It means we're going to fight it all the harder because our stake in the future is so big. We can win our fight without the Communists and we don't want their help." In the end, the Robeson-Robinson conflict boiled down to two men who knew racism first hand. Robeson had seen too many closed doors in America to believe American politicians would open them. Robinson had seen one door cracked open, and it had given him faith in the system.

RETREAT FROM THE INDIAN NEW DEAL

More than anything else, the rise of the Cold War precipitated dramatic changes in U.S. Indian policy. During the 1930s and World War II, the so-called Indian New Deal of President Franklin D. Roosevelt had ended a century of assimilationist crusading on the part of the federal government. The Indian New Deal—embodied in the Indian Reorganization Act of 1934, the Oklahoma Indian Welfare Act of 1935, and the Alaska Reorganization Act of 1937—had praised the virtues of cultural diversity, restored political power to tribal governments, and terminated the allotment program, which had alienated tens of millions of acres of Indian land. Most Native American leaders had hailed the legislation as a new day in Indian affairs.

But in the immediate postwar years, a conservative mood blanketed the country. The twin shocks of the Great Depression and World War II had upset the national equilibrium, and many Americans yearned for simpler times when the pace of change had been slower and values more constant. Some critics of federal Indian policy argued that the Indian New Deal, by perpetuating cultural differences, had been un-American and inconsistent with the traditional melting pot ideology that had always placed a high premium on assimilation. They also criticized John Collier, commissioner of Indian affairs under FDR, for being too liberal, perhaps even a political radical.

At the same time, economic interest groups in the West had tried to get at reservation land—to turn it into large commercial farms or resort developments—in short, to make money off the land. But the federal government's trust policy and the Indian Reorganization Act prevented that. Western congressmen wanted to repeal the Indian Reorganization Act, dissolve the tribes as legal and corporate entities, and end the federal trust status of tribal land, which prevented White economic interests from purchasing it. The new objectives of conservatives, in both Congress and at the state and local level, became assimilating Native Americans and then exploiting reservation land.

As a prerequisite to dissolving reservations and tribal governments, conservatives wanted to resolve all outstanding Indian claims against the federal government. Throughout U.S. history, the government had regularly reneged on treaty arrangements, illegally seized Indian land, and forced Indian peoples to move. Many Indian activists demanded monetary compensation for their losses, and in 1946 Congress passed the Indian Claims Commission Act, which established an Indian Claims Commission (ICC) to adjudicate tribal claims and assess compensation. To secure compensation for lost lands, timber rights, and mineral rights, tribes had to prove that they had occupied the land in question "from time immemorial" and that the federal government had intentionally violated treaty arrangements. If such a case could be made, they deserved compensation, so the legislation went. All claims had to be filed by 1951.

Native Americans quickly filed 852 claims totaling $1.2 billion in damages. The federal government hoped to wrap up all of the claims within a decade and get on with the business of assimilating the Indians, but the process proved more difficult; sorting out the various claims became a legal no-man's land of confusion, competition, and hyperbole. Most of the claims argued that the federal government had undervalued the land at the time of the initial treaty arrangement. A tribal official of the Seminole people labeled the Indian Claims Commission Act a "full employment law for White lawyers and White accountants." Tribes filing claims first had to prove to the ICC that they had actually occupied the land for centuries or even millennia, but such claims proved difficult to establish because most tribes had moved from region to region over the course of decades and centuries. Once tribal sovereignty over the land was established, lawyers had to prove that the Indians had lost the land through legal chicanery, and accountants had to place a dollar value on the land at the time of its alienation. Those same accountants then scoured through Bureau of Indian Affairs records and added up the total value of all the food, medicine, clothing, and blankets the tribe had received over the years from the federal government. That amount was then subtracted from the award.

Finally, once an award had been made, tribes often engaged in internecine civil wars over how to distribute the money, with full-bloods wanting the funds to come en masse to the tribe and mixed-bloods wanting it in per capita cash payments. Intratribal relations often soured, and lawsuits flooded the federal courts. By 1959, the ICC had completed only a few dozen claims totaling $50 million, with the largest award—$32 million—going to the Ute Indians, and the smallest—$2,500—going to the Poncas. The whole claims process became bogged down in bureaucratic and legal maneuvering, and as late as 1978, when Congress closed down the ICC, it had settled only 285 of the original 852 claims filed, for a total of $800 million.

But conservatives in Congress were convinced that the compensation program, which represented one leg of the assimilationist public policy tripod, was proceeding well enough to justify implementation of the second leg: "termination." On August 1, 1953, Congress passed several termination resolutions: ending the federal government authority over Indian tribes; ending the "trust relationship" that defined Indians as wards of the federal government; naming Indians as full beneficiaries of their U.S. citizenship but also subjecting them to such obligations of state and local citizenship as tax liability and civil and criminal jurisdiction; and trading federal legal jurisdiction over reserva-

Photo by Arthur Rothstein; Library of Congress, Prints & Photographs Division, LC-USF34-029817-D

Native Americans picking radishes on a farm near Moapa Reservation, Nevada.

tion land for state and local jurisdiction. According to the logic of termination, Native Americans would be forced to interact with Whites in neighboring communities, and such interaction—economic, social, and legal—would begin the process of assimilating them into the larger society.

The Bureau of Indian Affairs did not implement termination all at once. The plan was to phase it in gradually, starting first with those tribes deemed most "ready" for it. The Indian peoples targeted first were the Utes and Paiutes of Utah, the Alabama-Coushattas of Texas, the Klamaths of Oregon, and the Menominees of Wisconsin. The results were disastrous. Between 1953 and 1956, Native Americans lost more than 1.6 million acres, most of it Klamath and Menominee land sold to pay state and local taxes or to enrich the pockets of mixed-blood Indians. White timber companies moved onto reservation land formerly held by Klamaths and Menominees and began clear-cutting. Tribal income fell dramatically, and most Klamaths and Menominees slipped into grinding poverty.

Termination quickly became a political hot potato for the Eisenhower administration, since Republican congressmen from the western states had played key roles in sponsoring the legislation. The National Congress of American Indians, an intertribal lobbying group formed in

1944 and representing dozens of tribes, bitterly denounced termination, as did such White-dominated civil rights groups as the American Indian Defense Association, the Association on American Indian Affairs, and the Indian Rights Association. In 1957, Ralph Nader, a student at Harvard Law School and editor of the *Harvard Law School Record,* wrote a highly influential article denouncing termination, and such liberal journals as *Harper's, The Nation,* and *Christian Century* joined the protest. Earl Old Person, head of the Blackfoot nation, captured Native American feelings about termination. "It is important to note," he said, "that in our Indian language the only translation for termination is to 'wipe out' or 'kill off'—. . . [H]ow can we plan our future when the Indian Bureau threatens to wipe us out as a race? It is like trying to cook a meal in your tipi when someone is standing outside trying to burn the tipi down."

President Eisenhower grew increasingly concerned about the emerging shift in public opinion; he correctly perceived that most Whites had some sympathy for the plight of Indian peoples. Toward the end of his first administration, the president put the brakes on termination, allowing the 1953 congressional resolutions to stand but forbidding the Bureau of Indian Affairs from terminating any more tribes. Termination remained on the law books but was no longer being enforced. The bitterness it had engendered would remain a part of federal-Indian relations for the next generation.

Relocation constituted the third leg of the assimilationist tripod. In 1950 President Harry Truman appointed Dillon S. Myer as Commissioner of Indian Affairs. During World War II, Myer had headed the War Relocation Authority (WRA), the federal agency responsible for implementing and supervising the incarceration of 110,000 Japanese Americans. An avowed assimilationist, Myer believed that America's ethnic problems would disappear only when ethnic minorities vanished into the larger population. Beginning in mid-1944, Myer began releasing from WRA camps those Japanese Americans who agreed to settle east of the Mississsippi River rather than back in their West Coast communities. He also made sure that the Japanese Americans departing the WRA camps did not concentrate in any particular region of the East, requiring them to scatter widely. Myer was convinced that they were far more likely to assimilate through intermarriage back east than in California. For Myer, the United States would become a stable, perfect society only when minority groups no longer existed as functional ethnic groups.

Later, as Commissioner of Indian Affairs, Myer took that approach to Native Americans. Traditional U.S. government policy, Myer argued, had kept Indian peoples isolated from other Americans on reservations, where assimilation became impossible. Reservation life, Myer was convinced, perpetuated tribal isolation and tribal traditions.

The solution, he decided, was to convince large numbers of Indians to leave the reservations and resettle in the cities. Myer became committed to what he called the relocation policy: convincing Native Americans to abandon the reservation for a new life in such cities as Los Angeles, Albuquerque, Dallas, Tulsa, Denver, Phoenix, and Salt Lake City. In the cities, Indian children could attend integrated public schools, Indian families could live in integrated neighborhoods and apartment houses, and Indian workers could find jobs in integrated industries. Over time, Myer was certain, urban and suburban Indians would lose their cultural ties to the tribe, abandon the Indian language, forget about the reservation, and live in a White world. Eventually, he believed, they would cease to exist as an ethnic community, disappearing into the White majority.

Relocation was implemented voluntarily beginning in 1951. Agents from the Bureau of Indian Affairs identified those Indian families most likely to succeed off the reservation and offered cash payments to relocate. More than 35,000 people agreed to participate. Bureau agents located housing in the cities, placed relocatees in jobs, provided a month's spending money, and then forgot about them, expecting assimilation to take place smoothly and quietly. Glib and self-satisfied, Myer remarked to a journalist in 1952, "I think I have solved the Indian problem. It's taken us three centuries to realize that all Indians need is to live like the rest of us and they'll be happy."

But they were not happy. The relocated Native Americans experienced severe culture shock in the cities. Cut off from their families and the extended relationships available in the tribe, they often felt lonely and isolated. Indian children in the public schools frequently experienced racial discrimination from White teachers and students who did not understand them. Urban life seemed impersonal and strange, completely different from the rhythms of reservation life. Unemployment and alcoholism soon plagued the relocated Indians, and school dropout rates were high. Many drifted back to the reservations, hoping to be left alone to live out their lives.

The crusade during the late 1940s and 1950s to assimilate Native Americans proved to be a dismal failure, but ironically it also planted the seeds of a Native American activism that would eventually blossom into the Red Power movement of the late 1960s and 1970s. Because of the termination controversy, a sea change occurred in Native American leadership. Until the 1950s, White liberals had dominated the drive to right the wrongs of the past. Such groups as the American Indian Defense Association and the Indian Rights Association, though professing to promote the needs of Native Americans, were nevertheless upper middle-class White groups who, for all their sympathies, could not identify with Indian needs. But in the protest over compensation, termination, and relocation, the National Congress of American Indians (NCAI) moved to the forefront of Indian activism. A lobbying group representing dozens of tribes and composed overwhelmingly of Indian members and Indian leaders, the NCAI became the most powerful activist group in Native America, largely displacing Whites as the voice of reform in Indian affairs.

The assimilationist crusade of the 1950s also sowed the seeds of a pan-Indian political movement. Throughout U.S. history, bitter tribal rivalries had prevented Native Americans from forming successful political or military coalitions. European settlers had always been able to overwhelm indigenous resistance, and divide-and-conquer tactics had led to the allotment program in the 1880s. But in the late 1940s and 1950s, the beginnings of pan-Indian activism could be seen. The National Congress of American Indians was the country's first truly pan-Indian organization, representing most of the country's major tribes, and its vocal opposition to termination and relocation gave it a heady political profile that garnered considerable political attention. Henceforth, when Congress or Bureau of Indian Affairs bureaucrats pondered changes in U.S. Indian policy, they would have to clear it with the National Congress of American Indians and secure NCAI support.

The NCAI demonstrated its new influence in 1958 when the U.S. Army Corps of Engineers tried to construct Kinzua Dam and flood thousands of acres of Seneca land in western New York. The Senecas protested bitterly, and conservatives in Congress tried a quid pro quo, promising to stop construction if the Senecas would agree to be terminated. The Senecas enlisted the support of the National Congress of American Indians, which successfully blocked the project and the termination attempt.

A pan-Indian spirit also arose in the cities of the Southwest and Midwest. Dillon S. Myer's relocation program had moved tens of thousands of full-blooded Indians to such cities as Los Angeles, Phoenix, and Chicago, where most of them had experienced serious social and political problems. But in addition to the Native Americans relocated under Myer's direction, tens of thousands of other Indians, mostly mixedbloods, had voluntarily settled in the cities, where they could find work and their children could receive good educations in public schools. Although they associated with Whites at some levels, as Myer had predicted, they were more likely to interact with other Indians, and as they interacted, specific tribal loyalties tended to lose significance. Urban Indians began to acquire a generic identity as Indians, and when they married across tribal lines, that pan-Indian identity deepened. When the militant Red Power first emerged late in the 1960s, it would trace its roots to the beginnings of the pan-Indian movement in the late 1940s and early 1950s.

The outline of pan-Indian activism first appeared in 1961 at the American Indian Chicago Conference. During the 1950s, slowly and gradually, the National Congress of American Indians became divided because of intertribal rivalries between Great Plains and Oklahoma Indians and between traditional leaders and a new, younger generation of urban pan-Indian leaders. More than 500 Indians from sixty-seven tribes gathered in Chicago to address these divisions. They issued a "Declaration of Indian Purpose":

> We believe in the inherent rights of all people to retain spiritual and cultural values. . . . Indians exercised this inherent right to live their own lives for thousands of years before the white man came and took their lands. . . . When Indians speak of the continent they yielded, they are not referring only to the loss of some millions of acres in real estate. They have in mind that the land supported a universe of things they knew, valued, and loved. With that continent gone, except for the few parcels they still retain, the basis of life is precariously held, but they mean to hold the scraps and parcels as earnestly as any small nation or ethnic group has ever determined to hold to identity and survival.

Conference leaders hoped the Kennedy administration would pick up on their demands for cultural survival and preserve the tribal land base.

But a younger generation of delegates found the "Declaration of Indian Purpose" too cautious and conservative. They were convinced that the leaders of the National Conference of American Indians had sold out to European Americans who controlled the Bureau of Indian Affairs. Raised and educated in the cities and endowed with a pan-Indian point of view, they rejected NCAI traditions. The young rebels were led by Clyde Warrior, an Oklahoma Ponca; Melvin Thom, a Nevada Paiute; and Herbert Blatchford, a New Mexico Navajo. Several months after the Chicago conference, they reconvened at the Gallup Indian Community Center in Gallup, New Mexico, and formed the National Indian Youth Council. In their "Statement of Policy," they argued that

> the weapons employed by the dominant society have become subtler and more dangerous than guns—these, in the form of educational, religious, and social reform, have attacked the very centers of Indian life by attempting to replace native institutions with those of the white man. . . . The major problem in Indian affairs is that the Indian has been neglected in determining the direction of programs and monies to Indian communities. It has always been white people or white-oriented institutions determining what Indian problems are and how to correct them. . . . Tribal people . . . need only the proper social and economic opportunities to establish any government policies affecting themselves. The Indian problem is the white man.

During the 1960s and 1970s, the National Indian Youth Council would play a key role in defining Native American concerns, including control of the Bureau of Indian Affairs, hunting and fishing rights, civil liberties and voting rights, and protection of Indian habitats.

REDS AND REFUGEES

Between 1945 and 1965, U.S. immigration policy and ethnic history became inseparably intertwined with U.S. foreign policy. World War II had destroyed the European economy, leaving millions of people destitute and hundreds of thousands homeless; many Americans, their own economy thriving, felt a sense of responsibility to ameliorate overseas suffering. During the Truman administration, Congress established the Marshall Plan to reconstruct the European economies and passed several pieces of legislation to permit the immigration of European refugees. Political support for Europeans displaced by the war was especially strong in the Northeast and upper Midwest, where immigrants from Poland, Italy, Germany, Greece, Lithuania, Latvia, Estonia, Romania, Bulgaria, Czechoslovakia, and Yugoslavia worried about their countrymen in the Old World.

On December 22, 1945, President Truman took note of their concerns and by executive order allowed 42,000 European refugees to immigrate to the United States. During World War II, so many GIs stationed overseas had married foreign women that special legislation was needed to bring them to the United States. The War Bride Act of 1946 provided for the immigration of 120,000 wives and children of American servicemen. But even these numbers were inadequate, given the number of refugees seeking a home in the United States. In June 1948, Congress passed the Displaced Persons Act, which provided for the immigration of another 205,000 displaced Europeans. Political pressure continued to mount in Congress, and in June 1950 new authorization was passed for the issuance of 341,000 visas and then 60,000 more in 1952.

Ironically, although most Americans had been horrified by the Holocaust, the refugee legislation of the late 1940s discriminated against Jewish refugees, making it extremely difficult, if not possible, for them to secure visas. Because their legal status had been disrupted by World War II, the Holocaust, and the destruction of identity papers, they faced insurmountable obstacles proving citizenship, and anti-Semitism did little to motivate Congress to provide exceptions to the law. It was not until 1950 that amendments to the Displaced Persons Act ended the discrimination against Jews.

In addition to the aftereffects of World War II, the advent of the Cold War affected U.S. immigration policy. When Mao Tse-tung and the

Chinese Communists triumphed and established the People's Republic of China, a stream of refugees poured out of the country into Hong Kong, and many of them wanted to move on to the United States. Political dissidents also fled eastern Europe when the Soviet Union lowered the Iron Curtain in the late 1940s. In 1953, Congress passed the Refugee Relief Act, which provided, in addition to regular immigration quotas, for the emergency immigration of an extra 186,000 political refugees from Communist countries. Between 1946 and 1955, a total of 406,028 immigrants entered the United States as "displaced" people.

The refugee problem and Cold War rivalry between the United States and the Soviet Union and People's Republic of China led to the first comprehensive reform of immigration legislation since the National Origins Act of 1924. The McCarran-Walter Act of 1952 retained the existing quota system, which favored immigrants from western Europe over immigrants from eastern Europe, Africa, and Asia, but it lifted the ban on immigration from China and Japan. In a world where the United States and the Soviet Union were marketing the virtues of their respective political and economic systems, American immigration policy could no longer afford to discriminate so explicitly against Asians. The McCarran-Walter Act also prohibited the immigration of Communists, radicals, and anarchists and provided for the deportation of Communist immigrants, even if they had earned U.S. citizenship. Convinced that the law's provisions for the deportation of Communists was unconstitutional, President Truman vetoed the McCarran-Walter bill, but Congress overrode the veto and it became law.

Global politics soon presented the United States with a new body of political refugees. In 1956, Hungarian freedom fighters rebelled against the Communist-puppet government imposed on them by the Soviet Union after World War II. Soviet Premier Nikita Khrushchev had little patience with the rebels, and he ordered Soviet troops and tanks to invade Budapest and crush the rebellion. The rebels fought back with Molotov cocktails and small-scale guerrilla action, but they were no match for the Russians. When it became obvious that the rebellion could not succeed, many rebels fled Hungary for Austria and then made their way west.

Newspaper headlines and television broadcasts in the United States made heroes and martyrs out of the Hungarian rebels; images of them stalking Soviet tanks with homemade bombs ignited enormous sympathy in the United States, and Americans were prepared to welcome the freedom fighters with open arms. Late in 1956, Congress passed legislation offering permanent visas to tens of thousands of Hungarian refugees, most of them representing the educated elite of their country.

During the 1950s, a total of 1,492,215 legal immigrants arrived from Europe—including 345,450 from Germany, 208,872 from the United Kingdom, 187,904 from Italy, and 127,985 from Poland. A total of 157,081 immigrants came from Asia during the decade. Immigrants from North America totaled 769,147, with 319,312 from Mexico, 274,926 from Canada, and 78,330 from Cuba. South America sent 72,166 immigrants to the United States and Africa a total of 16,569.

THE HISPANIC MOSAIC

The booming American economy and the Cold War also stimulated new waves of Spanish-speaking immigrants to the United States. After World War II, millions of Mexicans crossed the border as virtual economic refugees. Between 1940 and 1955, the population growth rate in Mexico increased from 2.1 percent a year to 2.4 percent, but the Mexican economy could not absorb the extra workers. At the same time, the U.S. economy faced a dramatic shortage of agricultural workers. World War II had increased the demand for factory labor, and long-term urbanization trends continued to pull people out of rural areas and into cities. Declines in immigration from Europe exacerbated the tight agricultural labor market.

Commercial farmers began to lobby for solutions. Plenty of potential workers were available in Mexico, but many Americans resisted allowing them to immigrate as permanent residents. Among southern congressmen, racial and religious bias against dark-skinned, Roman Catholic Mexicans ran high. Many Whites in the Southwest harbored similar fears. The only solution that had any political legs to stand on was permitting short-term, temporary work visas. In 1942 Congress authorized the *bracero* (work hands) program, which extended temporary visas to Mexican laborers willing to work seasonally on farms and railroads. They would arrive in the largest numbers in the summer and fall (especially in California, Arizona, New Mexico, Colorado, and Texas) when crops were harvested and then head home for winter and early spring. The AFL-CIO, Teamsters' Union, and the railroad brotherhoods vigorously protested the *bracero* program, insisting that it would drive down wages and eliminate jobs for American workers. George Meany, head of the AFL-CIO, labeled the *bracero* program an "affront to every American working family. The growers want to enrich themselves at the expense of the working poor." Commercial growers disagreed. In 1956, a California grape farmer said, "How can it take away American jobs when I can't get American workers to sign up. If I left my fields to American workers, my grapes would rot on the vine."

Throughout the next twenty years, the *bracero* program brought more than 5 million Mexican workers to the United States. In addition, millions of Mexicans not included in the *bracero* program immigrated illegally, becoming the country's most exploited workers. Afraid of being deported by the Immigration and Naturalization Service (INS), they could not complain about working conditions, and employers consistently defied existing minimum wage and maximum hours legislation, paying them as little as the market would bear. The problem of illegal Mexican immigration became so controversial, and the demands of labor unions so intense, that in 1954 the INS launched Operation Wetback, a massive program to deport undocumented Mexican workers. By the time the crusade was over, more than 1 million Mexican workers had been forced back to Mexico, with Mexican American community leaders often howling in protest because of heavy-handed INS tactics.

The political agitation between growers and union leaders continued unabated, but in 1965, with Democrat Lyndon B. Johnson in the White House and Democrats in control of Congress, the labor unions prevailed, and Congress ended the *bracero* program. During the previous two decades, however, millions of Mexican workers had learned how to enter the United States, how to travel, how to find work, and how to avoid detection, so the end of the *bracero* program marked the beginning of massive increases in illegal immigration from Mexico. By that time, the Mexican American population of the United States stood at approximately 8 million, nearly triple what it had been at the outbreak of World War II. In 1965, only one in ten Americans of Mexican descent could trace his or her ancestry back to the original Hispanic settlers of California, New Mexico, and Texas.

Puerto Rican immigrants also flocked to the United States during the late 1940s, 1950s, and early 1960s. The U.S. job market attracted Puerto Ricans who suffered from endemic poverty and high rates of unemployment. The United States had acquired Puerto Rico from Spain after the Spanish-American War, and in 1917 Congress awarded Puerto Ricans U.S. citizenship. As U.S. citizens, Puerto Ricans were free of immigration laws and could come to the mainland at will. Inexpensive one-way plane tickets between San Juan and New York City made the journey relatively simple. Like Mexican *braceros,* thousands of Puerto Ricans originally worked commercial farms from Florida to Massachusetts as contract laborers, but most Puerto Rican immigrants eventually settled in cities, especially New York City's urban ghettoes—the Bronx, the South Bronx, the Lower East Side, Spanish Harlem, and the Williamsburg section of Brooklyn. By 1965, more than 1.2 million Puerto Ricans lived on the mainland, compared to only 2.8 million on the island itself.

Cuban Americans constituted the third major Hispanic immigrant group in the United States. A small Cuban emigré community has been in Florida and New York City ever since the late nineteenth century, but massive Cuban immigration did not begin until 1959, when

Fidel Castro ousted Cuban dictator Fulgencio Batista and took over the country. Once a popular figure in U.S. policy circles, Castro quickly disillusioned and then terrified most Americans by proclaiming himself a Communist, nationalizing American-owned property on the island, redistributing land among the peasants, and conducting a campaign of political terror against former followers of Batista.

The Dwight D. Eisenhower administration, positively apoplectic about having a Communist nation so close to home, decided to bring down the Castro regime. In an attempt to destroy the Cuban economy, Eisenhower announced an embargo of all American exports to Cuba and outlawed the importation of Cuban sugar. The Soviet Union then filled the breach, buying up Cuban sugar and supplying Cuba with hundreds of millions of dollars in foreign aid, enough to keep the Cuban economy afloat and place the island firmly within the Soviet sphere of influence. When John F. Kennedy took office in 1961, the U.S. assault on the Castro regime assumed more direct, militaristic dimensions. In April 1961, an army of 1,500 anti-Castro Cuban refugees, trained in Guatemala by the Central Intelligence Agency, invaded Cuba at the Bay of Pigs. It was a military fiasco, and Castro's forces managed to scuttle the invasion and capture the misfit commandos in a matter of days. President Kennedy accepted full responsibility for the disaster, and Castro crowed to all who would listen about his victory over the United States.

Although Cuban peasants idolized Fidel Castro, his popularity among the Cuban middle and upper classes had plummeted as soon as he started to confiscate private property. The 1,500 Cuban refugees who had participated in the Bay of Pigs invasion had been a vanguard of unhappy Cubans ready to emigrate to the United States. Discontent in Cuba among small businesspeople, commercial farmers, and corporate employees—all of whom had much to lose in the transition to a socialist economy—became contagious, and emigration from the island accelerated. Some arrived on authorized refugee airlifts from Havana to Miami, while others risked the shark-infested waters of the Florida Straits in motorboats, dinghies, and rafts. By 1965, the exodus had brought 250,000 Cubans to the United States, most of whom settled in south Florida, where they became rabidly anti-Castro, anti-Communist Republicans as they plotted new ways to overthrow Fidel Castro and return to the island.

At first Castro encouraged the emigration as a means of ridding himself of political opposition, but the exodus represented an enormous opportunity cost to Cuba. The vast majority of the early Cuban immigrants were lawyers, accountants, engineers, technicians, physicians, dentists, and teachers—the educated infrastructure of the entire economy. And Cuba's loss would be America's gain. The immigrants transformed the economy of south Florida and began a process that would make Miami the commercial center for all of Latin America.

IMMIGRATION REFORM

During the early 1960s, the inadequacies of the McCarran-Walter Act of 1952 became more and more clear, and demands for immigration policy reform intensified. The rush of displaced persons and political refugees had resulted in a reactive U.S. immigration policy, and many critics began to demand reform legislation. At the same time, the civil rights movement had discredited all forms of color prejudice and racism. Because the McCarran-Walter Act had retained the old quota system, which had long been biased in favor of northern and western Europeans and against eastern and southern Europeans, Asians, and Africans, many civil rights activists considered the law an anachronism from the country's racist past. Finally, immigration patterns had begun to change. European immigration began to decline rapidly, whereas immigration from Asia, Africa, and South America increased dramatically. European countries were often not even filling their annual quotas of America-bound immigrants; Asian quotas, on the other hand, could not come near to meeting demand.

Agricultural economics in the United States also dictated immigration policy reform. Congress had ended the *bracero* program in 1965, and large commercial farmers in the Southwest worried about whether they would be able to hire sufficient workers to harvest their crops. They applied political pressure in Congress for a new immigration law that would permit substantial immigration from Mexico.

On December 1, 1965, Congress passed and President Johnson signed the Immigration and Nationality Act, the first major revision of U.S. immigration policy since 1924. The law ended the forty-year-old system of ethnic quotas based on ethnic origins. The United States would permit a total of 170,000 people from the eastern hemisphere to immigrate each year, except that no more than 20,000 people could come from any one country. Preferences went to refugees, those with family members already in the United States, and professional and skilled workers. The act also, for the first time in U.S. history, limited immigration from the western hemisphere to 120,000 people per year, and they were allowed to enter on a first-come, first-served basis without categorical preference or limits from any given country. Such a provision guaranteed enough Mexican immigrant workers to work the large commercial farms.

Passage of the Immigration and Nationality Act of 1965 ended an era in American immigration history. Ever since 1882, when Congress passed the Chinese Exclusion Act, U.S. immigration policy had been rife with racism, with light-skinned Europeans enjoying preferential treatment and darker-skinned people encountering prejudice and discrimination. On the law books, at least, immigration policy had become color-blind, and the Statue of Liberty's promise—"Give me your huddled masses, yearning to be free"—once again had a chance of being realized.

Part

II

———

RUMBLINGS OF DISCONTENT, 1965–1980

In July 1964, when Congress passed and President Lyndon B. Johnson signed the Civil Rights Act of 1964, civil rights activists hailed the legislation as a new day in U.S. history, a watershed moment in which the full promise of the Declaration of Independence and the Bill of Rights could finally be realized in the life of every American. The crusading zeal of such organizations as the Southern Christian Leadership Conference, the National Association for the Advancement of Colored People, and the Student Nonviolent Coordinating Committee had obliterated the last vestiges of *de jure* discrimination. Every U.S. citizen would now be able to compete on a level playing field according to the same rules. The legal obstacles erected to keep African Americans and other minorities confined to poverty and second-class status had gone the way of powdered wigs, horses and buggies, and silent films.

The burst of optimism and euphoria proved to be naive. Racism ran deep in the veins of American society, and no set of Supreme Court decisions or laws of Congress could cleanse it immediately. Formal, recognized forms of discrimination might no longer possess legal legs on which to stand, but institutionalized racism was alive and well, buried in the psyches of tens of millions of Americans. Overcoming it—changing the hearts and minds of an entire country—would prove to be daunting.

Just how difficult it would be became abundantly clear on July 18, 1964, just two weeks after the Civil Rights Act became law. New York

City exploded in racial rebellion. A city police officer had shot and killed James Powell, a 15-year-old boy, and many African Americans believed the police had used excessive force. Police brutality had long been an issue in New York City because of the large number of White police officers who patrolled Black neighborhoods. A grand jury refused to indict the police officer, but local officials from the Congress of Racial Equality (CORE) demanded that he be fired. The New York City Police Department refused and simply transferred the officer to administrative duty. At a CORE rally in Harlem protesting police brutality, activists marched on the local police precinct headquarters. Speakers from CORE urged the crowd to take action, and as police set up barricades, fighting broke out. Enraged, rampaging demonstrators threw rocks, hurled bottles, and looted some stores. Only warning shots fired by police kept the crowd from invading the precinct offices.

The situation then deteriorated rapidly throughout the city. At the funeral services for the young man, Jesse Gray, a Black nationalist, called on crowds to take power into their hands to punish the city for what it had done to Black people. More than 1,000 African American rioters then hit the streets in Brooklyn, Harlem, and Bedford-Stuyvesant. The rioting continued for four days and resulted in twenty-five dead, 140 injured, 112 looted stores, 556 property damage reports, and 276 arrests. Police did not manage to rein in the rioting until July 22. In the meantime, the newspaper and television media broadcast images of rioting Blacks, burning buildings, and looted stores to the entire world. So much for a new day in American race relations.

During the next twenty years, Americans would struggle with issues of race and ethnicity, trying to cope with their diversity while remaining faithful to the Declaration of Independence's conviction that "all men are created equal . . . [and] . . . are endowed by their Creator with certain unalienable Rights, that among these are Life, Liberty, and the pursuit of Happiness." As the civil rights movement expanded from African Americans to include Hispanics and Native Americans, and as the battle against institutional racism produced affirmative action and school busing as its key strategies, the political coalition of African Americans, Jews, socialists, liberals, and White union workers that had brought to pass the Civil Rights Act of 1964 and the Voting Rights Act of 1965 disintegrated. Civil rights debates became more and more shrill and vitriolic. When he led a civil rights march in Cicero, Illinois, in 1966, Martin Luther King, Jr., encountered unanticipated resistance and animosity from local Whites, which was perhaps even worse than what he had experienced in the South. "I think the people of Mississippi ought to come to Chicago," he later said, "to learn how to hate."

Chapter Four

BLACK AND HISPANIC MILITANCY

The New York City riots of July 1964 were only a rehearsal for larger and bloodier racial conflagrations that swept through the country in the late 1960s. The riots or racial rebellions heralded the end of Martin Luther King's nonviolent civil disobedience. On August 11, 1965, a White police officer working the Watts section of Los Angeles arrested Marquette Frye, a young Black man. Relations between the White police and Black residents of Watts were no better than those between White cops and Black residents in New York City, and Black activists frequently raised the specter of police brutality. When the police tried to place Frye in custody and push him into the squad car, a crowd of his family members and friends gathered and denounced the police officers. The police called for backup, and a dozen squad cars arrived, lights flashing, brakes screeching, and sirens blaring.

As police bolted out of their cars with billy clubs and shotguns, more Black residents of Watts surrounded the cars. Rocks, bricks, and bottles began to rain on the police, and many of them, without riot gear, were injured in the melee. Like a prairie wildfire, the rioting spread rapidly from block to block. Once local television news crews were on the scene, the rioting resembled spontaneous combustion, breaking out like flash fires throughout African American neighborhoods. Unlike New York City police, the Los Angeles cops could not control the crowds.

By the early morning hours of August 12, the rioters had started looking beyond the police for targets. An estimated 7,000 Black youths, egged on by many adults, fabricated torches and Molotov cocktails and began burning down stores, but not before looting them. Images of young Black men and women lugging televisions, chairs, radios, record players, beer, whiskey, and wine from stores made headlines nationwide. Some businesses and property bearing signs like "Negro Owned," "Blood," or "Brother" escaped the mob, and many with such signs did not survive. Some of the rioters broke into gun shops and pilfered rifles, pistols, and ammunition and then hid out on rooftops and began sniping at police. Some White motorists who accidentally drove into Watts were accosted and beaten and their vehicles burned.

Throughout the rest of the city, frightened Whites headed to gun stores and armed themselves in panicky self-defense. By the evening of August 12, one gun store owner in a well-to-do section of Santa Monica told a journalist, "I don't have a rifle, pistol, or bee-bee gun left or a single round of ammunition. People are wild-eyed and terrified; it looks like we're going to have a real race war unless somebody gets a handle on this." Governor Pat Brown of California telephoned President Johnson and confessed defeat. The riot was out of control.

Johnson acted quickly. On August 16, he deployed 10,000 National Guard troops to Watts; they arrived in armored personnel carriers and armed to the teeth. Along with another 5,000 police officers from Los Angeles and surrounding communities, they cordoned off a 46-square-mile area of the city and patrolled it like an invading army. Smoke from hundreds of burning buildings rose up and was carried inland by ocean breezes. Those residents of Los Angeles who didn't see any rioting could certainly smell it. One older National Guardsman, who had served under General Douglas MacArthur in the assault on Luzon in the Philippines during World War II, remarked, "This isn't much different than fighting the Japs, but it's in my own damned country. I can't believe it."

Los Angeles resembled a police state—complete with curfews, uniformed patrols, road-blocked streets, and documents inspections. After several days, the riot petered out, but the damage statistics told a grisly tale. Thirty-four people were dead and 1,032 injured, with 4,000 people arrested and $40 million in property damage. Even more damage had been inflicted on the civil rights coalition. The Watts riot terrified millions of White Americans and robbed many of their sympathies for the plight of Black people. America would never be the same again.

BLACK POWER

In 1964, when Congress passed the Civil Rights Act, the fledgling civil rights movement had achieved a major victory. Along with a series of Supreme Court decisions in the late 1940s and 1950s, Jim Crow segregation was dead, on the law books at least. Its last vestige died on June 12, 1967, when the Supreme Court decided the *Loving v. Virginia* case. Virginia state law prohibited interracial marriages, but the court overturned the law, arguing that it violated the equal protection and due process clauses of the Fifth and Fourteenth Amendments. The right to choose a marriage partner, the court concluded, could not be infringed upon by the state. In 1967, the civil rights movement achieved another milestone when President Johnson appointed Thurgood Marshall as the first African American justice in Supreme Court history.

But despite such judicial, legislative, and executive victories, the African American community still faced poverty, *de facto* segregation, and institutional racism. As Whites fled to the suburbs, many businesses relocated outside the city, making it more difficult for African Americans to find work. At the same time the U.S. economy was shifting from a manufacturing to a service base; blue-collar jobs were steadily decreasing as white-collar ones became more plentiful. But white-collar jobs required education and technical skills, and large numbers of underprivileged African Americans did not qualify. Although earlier immigrants had used unskilled urban jobs as the bootstrap out of the ghettoes, Blacks no longer had those choices. They were trapped in a changing economy and a deteriorating physical environment, and their poverty became more and more serious. In 1970 more than one in three African American families functioned below the poverty line, and the median Black income was only about 60 percent that of Whites. Unemployment was twice as high as for White workers, and joblessness for African American teenagers reached more than 40 percent in some cities during the 1970s.

A younger generation of impatient Black leaders reacted with the Black Power movement. The shift to Black Power appeared in two guises: one spontaneous and emotional, the other deliberate and ideological. The New York City Black uprising of 1964 and the Watts rebellion of 1965 were opening chapters in a series of urban racial conflagrations in the late 1960s. In 1967, Newark, New Jersey, erupted. After Black taxi cab driver John Smith was arrested, false rumors spread through the Black community that he had been beaten to death. This news, coupled with the defeat of a Black city council candidate and the proposed development of a medical college on a site wanted by Blacks for more housing, resulted in a riot from July 12–17, 1967. Approximately 3,000 rioters gained control of downtown Newark and the West, East, and Central Wards. A spirit of cooperation developed among the rioters, who formed human chains to more easily remove stolen goods from the stores. As in Watts, the National Guard had to be deployed. Almost 5,000 police officers and soldiers worked to secure the perimeter, enforce martial law, and distribute emergency food rations to the community. After five days of chaotic fighting, the officers were tired, and several incidents of "friendly fire" occurred. After six days, the rioting came to an end. Every business in the riot zone was damaged in some manner; business losses exceeded $35 million. Casualties included twenty-six dead and 1,500 injured. Despite more than 1,500 arrests, only 2 percent of Newark's population was involved in the rioting.

One week later, Detroit exploded. Between July 23 and July 30, forty-three people died, 2,000 were injured, and another 5,000 were left homeless. More than 7,000 people were arrested in rioting that covered downtown Detroit and a 7-mile radius. In all, property damage ranged from $250 to $500 million. The Detroit riot, however, was unique in several ways. First, it was biracial; both Blacks and Whites rioted together, not against one another. Second, citizens not involved in the rioting did not hide in their homes but helped firefighters by standing guard to protect them from the rioting. Also, the riot was not restricted to the ghettoes; looting and firebombing spread to the suburbs. Officials realized that this was not an ordinary riot; in addition to 8,000 National Guard troops, local officials requested federal military assistance.

By the end of the second day, President Johnson sent former Secretary of Defense Cyrus Vance to assess the situation; on July 24, the president announced on television that he had issued orders for federal troops to quell the rioting. Paratroopers and airborne divisions were deployed into Detroit and into Flint, Pontiac, and Grand Rapids, where other disturbances were beginning. Federal troops would fight for four days before rioting ceased. At the conclusion of the riot, media opinion turned against the officers. The media cited alleged police brutality, and the courts indicted three officers for misconduct. Although the officers were later exonerated, the media and the public no longer viewed police officers as heroes protecting society from evil elements.

Clearly, urban rioting had escalated over a three-year period from violent racial flareups to mass participation mayhem. Because of the riots, President Johnson established a Commission on Civil Disorder in 1967. Governor Otto Kerner of Illinois chaired the commission. In March 1968, the Kerner Report was issued. It denied that Communist subversion had anything to do with the riots and instead looked to domestic economic and social problems. Most rioters were unemployed young men who had dropped out of high school and who feared and/or hated the police. The report identified high urban crime rates, poverty, lack of educational opportunity, poor health facilities, poor ghetto services, and extremely high unemployment as the real causes of urban discontent. America could not expect an end to rioting until the causes of urban blight were addressed. The commission also agreed, however, that the media had grossly exaggerated the extent of the rioting. The Kerner Report identified 164 "racial disorders," of which eight were deemed "major" and thirty-three "serious." There was no evidence of a nationwide conspiracy to incite the riots. They were, on the other hand, spontaneous rebellions growing out of severe economic, social, and political problems in urban America.

In addition to spontaneous rioting to protest injustice, Black Power expressed itself ideologically during the late 1960s and early 1970s. The idea of Black Power was hardly new. The Black Muslims, founded by Elijah Muhammad in 1930, rose to national prominence in the early 1960s. Preaching the ultimate doom of "devil" Whites and the triumph of Blacks, the Black Muslims called for Black pride, Black enterprise, and a separate Black state. They also called on African Americans to think less about being nonviolent and more about returning violence for violence.

The earliest popular proponent of Black Power was Malcolm X. Born as Malcolm Little in Omaha, Nebraska, he was raised in Boston, where he got into trouble with the law. He earned a ten-year prison sentence for burglary, but in the penitentiary, he came upon the religious teachings of the Nation of Islam, and he soon converted. The conversion was deep and sincere. Upon his release from prison in 1952, Malcolm X moved to Detroit and became a follower of Elijah Muhammad. The last name of X was symbolic of the family name of his ancestors, whom he would never know because slavery had ripped his people from their African home. He was a charismatic preacher, telling Black people to discard the ghetto mentality, build strong marriages and families, and avoid pork, narcotics, alcohol, gambling, fornication, and adultery. By 1961, Malcolm X was named National Minister in the Nation of Islam.

In contrast to the nonviolent civil disobedience of Martin Luther King, Malcolm X urged Black people to defend themselves when necessary. He called King just another Uncle Tom. When President John F. Kennedy was assassinated, Malcolm called it a case of the chickens coming home to roost. To most White people, he appeared to be a dangerous firebrand. By that time, many Black Muslims believed Malcolm X was becoming too powerful. When Malcolm X learned that Elijah Muhammad was guilty of adultery with two of his secretaries, he broke with the Nation of Islam, founding his own organization— Muslim Mosque, Inc. In 1964, his life changed again when he made the Muslim pilgrimage to Mecca. There he discovered that Islam was color-blind and eschewed the racist teachings of the Nation of Islam. Malcolm returned to the United States as El-Hajj Malik El-Shabazz,

Civil rights leaders pose in front of the statue of Abraham Lincoln, at the Lincoln Memorial.

where he founded the Organization for African Unity, a group promoting Black nationalism regardless of religious persuasion. Malcolm X was assassinated in 1965 by a rival Black Muslim faction.

One year later, the phrase "Black Power" was seared into the national consciousness. James Meredith, the African American who had integrated the University of Mississippi in 1962, decided to prove just how much Mississippi had changed in four years, promising to march from Memphis, Tennessee, to Jackson, Mississippi, during voter registration week without harassment. One day into the march, however, he was wounded by a shotgun blast, and civil rights leaders from all over the country descended on Mississippi to complete the Freedom March. But while Martin Luther King, Jr., still spoke of nonviolent civil disobedience, Stokely Carmichael, the young leader of the Student Nonviolent Coordinating Committee (SNCC), startled the nation by ridiculing nonviolence and crying out for Black Power. A native of Trinidad who had been raised in New York City, Carmichael had participated in the Freedom rides of 1961 and had worked to register voters in Mississippi and Alabama. The racism he experienced left him equally contemptuous of southern conservatives and Black and White liberals. Carmichael urged Blacks to take matters into their own hands.

On the other side of the country, Huey Newton and Bobby Seale established the Black Panthers in Oakland, California, and called for

African American control of the ghettoes. Rejecting the middle-class values of White society and the nonviolent, civil disobedience tactics of mainstream civil rights organizations, the Black Panthers appealed to unemployed young Black young men living in urban ghettoes. They asserted the right to defend themselves against racist attacks by the White power structure, especially the police, imposed a militaristic discipline on members, advocated arming the Black community, and espoused a militant machismo philosophy.

Not surprisingly, armed conflict frequently occurred between Black Panthers and police. In Chicago, police killed Panther leaders Fred Hampton and Mark Clark during a raid. Bobby Seale and Huey Newton were indicted for shooting several policemen. Charges were dropped against Seale, but Newton was convicted and spent nearly two years in jail before the conviction was reversed on appeal. In 1968, Eldridge Cleaver, Black Panther minister of information, ran for president of the United States on the Peace and Freedom Party ticket. In 1969, their newspaper—*Black Panther*—had a circulation of 140,000. The Panthers espoused a philosophy of Black nationalism and tried to maintain breakfast programs for poor children in the ghettoes.

But there was also a negative side to the Black Panthers. Drug abuse was common, and Panther violence was too often gratuitous, directed at one another as well as at police. In most cities, the children's breakfast program was frequently based on extortion and racketeering, threatening to firebomb business establishments that did not contribute. And there were powerful antifeminist, antiwomen rhetoric and values among Black Panther leaders. Early in the 1970s, the Panthers rejected their emphasis on violence and tried to focus on political organization, but by then the group was in an advanced state of decline.

Philosophy professor Angela Davis employed a version of Black Power in her politics and gained notoriety in the late 1960 and early 1970s. A native of Alabama, Davis had been influenced by Marxist philosopher Herbert Marcuse during her undergraduate years at Brandeis University and later graduate work at the University of California at San Diego. She became active in the Student Nonviolent Coordinating Committee and took a teaching position at UCLA. In July 1968, Davis joined the Communist Party. The next year she traveled to Cuba, where she decided that African Americans had something in common with all Third World peoples. Later that year, Davis became a national figure when Governor Ronald Reagan of California fired her from the teaching post at UCLA on the grounds that she was a Communist.

By that time she was involved with defense of the Soledad brothers, one of whom was George Jackson, for murdering a prison guard. Jackson was killed trying to escape from San Quentin. On August 7, 1970, Jackson's younger brother Jonathan, using weapons registered in Davis's name, seized several hostages during a trial in Marin County. In a shootout that followed, Jackson murdered Judge Harold Haley before being killed by the police. Because Davis owned the weapons, she was charged with conspiracy to commit murder. Eventually, she was acquitted of the charges.

Despite the rhetoric of Black Power and the fear it sent through White America, the phrase meant different things to different people. To Whites, the slogan was incendiary, somehow implying that the social order was about to undergo revolutionary change. To the Congress of Racial Equality (CORE), Black Power meant direct political action through the Democratic Party and the mobilization of African American votes in the South. The Black Panthers and SNCC viewed it as community control; they demanded African American police and African American firemen in African American neighborhoods, African American teachers and principals in African American schools, and African American-owned businesses to serve the African American market. And to some radical groups, Black Power implied the use of retaliatory violence to end poverty and discrimination.

The rise of the Black Power movement, along with a growing sense of frustration over the suffering of Blacks in the United States, pushed Martin Luther King beyond civil rights to economic and foreign policy issues. Just how deeply American racism ran became abundantly clear to King in 1966 when he took the civil rights movement north to protest segregated neighborhoods. Because banks, savings and loan institutions, and mortgage companies regularly practiced redlining—refusing to make loans to Blacks to purchase homes in all-White neighborhoods—segregated housing was the rule in America. Many neighborhoods also had "residential covenants"—agreements among neighborhood residents not to sell homes to Blacks. Some city councils passed special zoning ordinances or complicated housing codes that made it cumbersome and difficult for Blacks to purchase homes in White neighborhoods. Renters had an equally difficult time because apartment owners in all-White complexes regularly refused to sign leases with minority families.

King targeted Chicago, where 90 percent of Black schoolchildren attended all-Black schools, even though no formal laws or regulations mandated it. African American children lived in neighborhoods where White people were never seen. Black public schools were overcrowded whereas White public schools had plenty of room. The reaction of local Whites was extraordinary. Thousands rallied to denounce King and demand that he leave their neighborhoods alone. The overt hostility surprised him. Even in Selma and Birmingham, Alabama, he had never encountered such vitriolic hatred. National Guard troops had to be called out to protect a few hundred Black protestors from

10,000 angry Whites. The Chicago demonstrations proved that White racism was a national, not just a southern problem.

King's stand against housing discrimination did yield one important result. President Johnson made it a civil rights issue. With the support of Senator Everett Dirksen of Illinois, who was the Republican minority leader in the Senate, Johnson pushed through Congress the Housing Act of 1968 and the Civil Rights Act of 1968. The Housing Act was designed to see to the construction of millions of new housing units in minority areas, whereas the Civil Rights Act struck down racially based residential covenants, attacked red-lining, and prohibited property owners with more than four rental units from discriminating against prospective renters on the basis of race.

King also entered the foreign policy arena. Early in 1965, he had developed serious misgivings about the Vietnam War, seeing it as a brutally misguided military campaign against a tiny, poor country that many perceived as simply another attempt by the White, industrialized West to colonize the rest of the world. King was also disturbed by the effect of the draft on the Black community and the inordinately large numbers of casualties Black soldiers were sustaining in 1965 and 1966. In 1967, he openly protested the Vietnam War and linked the civil rights and antiwar movements, a step that earned him the ire of President Johnson and most civil rights leaders, who worried that linking the two movements would only dissipate the force of the campaign for equality. But King was convinced that the Vietnam War was diverting financial and emotional resources away from domestic programs and into a futile effort abroad.

Another prominent figure felt the same way. Cassius Clay—a gifted athlete with unusual speed and quickness, given his size, and just 18—had won a gold medal for boxing at the 1960 Olympic Games. He returned home a national hero, and a consortium of local businessmen in Louisville, Kentucky, decided to finance his run for the heavyweight championship. Brash and outspoken, Clay fancied himself another Gorgeous George, the outlandish professional wrestler who preened before the press in elaborate outfits and bragged incessantly about his abilities. Clay bragged as well. The difference, of course, was that professional boxing was a real sport, and Clay was among the best ever to step into a ring. He finally got a shot at the title in 1964. The reigning champion was Sonny Liston, a man of few words whose reputation for ferocity was unmatched. Clay bragged about humiliating Liston in the ring, and the world waited for the young challenger to get what was coming to him. He did. Clay beat Liston unmercifully and won the heavyweight championship. The next day, Clay stunned the sports world by announcing his conversion to the Nation of Islam and the change of his name to Muhammad Ali. He defended his title against all comers. Outside the ring, he constantly had to defend his religious beliefs, which were sincere, against the criticisms of non-Muslims.

He soon found himself, however, reduced from sports icon to draft dodger. In 1966, when the selective service declared him eligible for the draft, Ali appealed for deferment as a religious conscientious objector, but the selective service rejected the request. Early in 1967, he announced that he would not go to war against the Vietnamese. "I ain't got no quarrel with those Vietcong, anyway," he said. "They never called me nigger." On April 18, 1967, he refused to take the oath and enter the U.S. Army. The World Boxing Association soon stripped him of his title, and in June 1967 a federal jury convicted him of draft evasion. Ali was sentenced to five years in prison and fined $10,000.

To African Americans and antiwar activists, Ali became a hero. At the time, he was 25 years old, at the peak of his athletic skills. State boxing commissions refused to issue him a license, and the State Department would not allow him to travel abroad. Unable to fight, Ali traveled widely throughout the country, making common cause with Martin Luther King in denouncing the Vietnam War and promoting the Nation of Islam. He appealed his case, and in June 1970 the U.S. Supreme Court overturned the conviction. Ali returned to the ring, regaining the heavyweight championship in October 1974. By that time, he had become the most recognizable person in the world and an icon to Black people everywhere.

When such Black activists as Muhammad Ali and Martin Luther King, Jr., denounced the Vietnam War, they acknowledged that racism affected every facet of American life—politics, society, economics, and foreign policy. King himself in 1968 turned to economics as his major focus when he called for a national crusade to eliminate poverty in America. He began preparing for a Poor People's March on Washington, DC, for the spring of 1968. He also decided to travel to Memphis, Tennessee, to lend support to a strike by garbage collectors who wanted better pay. Early in April, King arrived in Memphis and delivered several impassioned speeches to garbage workers, civil rights groups, and Black church congregations. But he was being stalked in Memphis by a violent racist intent on killing him. James Earl Ray was a poor drifter who blamed King for all of the problems in his personal life. On the afternoon of April 4, 1968, while King was relaxing on a balcony at his Memphis hotel, Ray took careful aim and put a bullet through the civil rights leader's neck. King died quickly and Ray fled.

News of the assassination spread within minutes across the United States. For tens of millions of African Americans, Martin Luther

King, Jr., had been the greatest leader of all time, and his death came first as a shock and then as a source of rage. Riots erupted throughout the country as Black people took their anger to the streets in an orgy of violence, as if their only way of coming to terms with King's death was through destruction and mayhem, and National Guard troops had to be widely deployed. Urban America in April 1968 resembled occupied America, a military state. James Earl Ray tried to flee the country but was apprehended in a matter of days. In a subsequent trial, he was convicted of murder and sentenced to life in prison.

King's death prompted a soul searching in Black America. Early in 1968, Harry Edwards of San Jose State University organized a boycott of the New York Athletic Club's annual track meet in Madison Square Garden. Because the club would not admit Blacks as members, Edwards argued that Black athletes should not compete in the meet. The boycott proved to be a success. A number of major African American track and field stars refused to compete, and the meet's attendance and television audiences declined dramatically.

Buoyed by his success with the New York Athletic Club, Edwards decided to launch a similar boycott of the 1968 Olympic Games in Mexico City. He made a simple argument: Why should Black athletes bring glory to a country that discriminates against them racially? Edwards organized the Olympic Project for Human Rights to supervise the boycott. He insisted that Black athletes all over the world refuse to compete unless these demands were met: the International Olympic Committee (IOC) ban South Africa and Rhodesia from the games until apartheid was destroyed; Avery Brundage was ousted as head of the IOC; Muhammad Ali had his boxing license restored; and Black coaches were added to the U.S. Olympic team. Brundage and the IOC at first tried to dig in and hold out, but Edwards had his first success when most Black African nations agreed to join the boycott. Mexico then decided to refuse admission into the country to any individual carrying South African or Rhodesian passports. In April 1968, the IOC caved in and banned South Africa and Rhodesia from all international competition.

Flushed with success, Edwards tried to keep the boycott going in the United States, because only one of his demands had been met. The assassination of Martin Luther King in April 1968 only made the urgency of the boycott more immediate. Throughout the spring and summer of 1968, Edwards traveled around the country speaking to Black athletes, trying to muster support for the boycott. To counter Edwards, the U.S. Olympic Committee sent the legendary Jesse Owens on a nationwide speaking tour, in which he argued against politicizing the Olympics. The boycott collapsed in the summer of 1968 when America's premier Black athletes decided to compete.

The boycott might have stalled, but Edwards's influence at Mexico City could not be denied. A number of African American athletes wore black socks during the Olympic trials and during the games as a symbolic protest. Tommy Smith and Juan Carlos placed first and third in the 200-meters race, and at the awards ceremony, when the "Star-Spangled Banner" was being played, they raised their arms in clenched, black-gloved fists in order "to give young African Americans something to be proud of, to identify themselves with." Their protest salute received major media coverage in the United States. So did boxer George Foreman's counter-salute. An African American from Houston, Foreman won the gold medal in heavyweight boxing. After the bout, he paraded around the ring, proudly waving an American flag.

Higher education became another battleground in the Black Power war. In 1969, Cornell University became ground zero in the conflict. Racial tensions had been growing on the campus, especially after a Black female student was expelled for refusing to lower the volume of the soul music she played in her dormitory room. A Jesuit professor was accused of being a racist. A group of Black students occupied the professor's office and then held his department chair and two secretaries hostage. When the incident ended, Cornell University President James Perkins refused to prosecute the Black students, arguing that they were just "trying to come to grips with the agonies of our society."

Perkins's failure to punish the students encouraged the militants, who then demanded immediate implementation of a Black studies program. When the university agreed to launch the program the next year, but not immediately, militant Black students invaded Perkins's office, destroyed books in the library, and demanded the establishment of an autonomous, degree-granting college at Cornell. They even physically attacked Perkins during a seminar on South African apartheid.

On April 18, 1969, White students placed a burning cross on the lawn of a Black sorority house. In response, Black militants invaded and seized control of the Cornell student union. A number of White fraternity students tried to recapture the building from the Blacks. Automatic weapons were smuggled to the Black students, and the Cornell administration capitulated, agreeing to establish the Black studies program and place it under the control of the militant students. When the Black students exited the student union after the agreement, they smiled and raised their weapons in triumph, with a legion of news photographers taking their pictures for broadcast and publication.

Many Black Power advocates also began to demand reparations— cash payments to Blacks for the suffering imposed on them by slavery and continuing racism. They took the idea of reparations from the

Treaty of Versailles ending World War I, when Allied leaders had officially blamed Germany for the war and imposed tens of billions of dollars in reparation payments. The militants hoped to use the demand for reparations to upstage more moderate Black leaders. The most spectacular moment in the campaign for reparations came in 1969 when James Forman, the new head of the Student Nonviolent Coordinating Committee, calmly walked to the pulpit—uninvited—in the middle of Sunday services at the Riverside Church in New York City and demanded that White churches offer up $500 million in reparations to compensate for centuries of racism. The speech earned Forman headlines in newspapers throughout the country, and the National Council of Churches responded by establishing fund-raising organizations to funnel money to disadvantaged groups. More traditional Black religious groups, such as the National Baptist Convention, roundly condemned Forman and the National Council of Churches for pandering to such a ridiculous demand, and little money ever found its way from White churches to the hands of poor Black people. The demand for reparations was, however, one of the more spectacular episodes in the history of the civil rights movement during the 1960s.

HISPANIC POWER

The Black Power movement inspired militancy among other minorities, including Hispanics. When the Immigration and Nationality Act of 1965 imposed an annual quota of 120,000 immigrants from the western hemisphere, the number of undocumented Mexican immigrants increased. Traditional push-pull forces could not be denied. Population growth in Mexico was staggering, and the labor market could not absorb all the workers. Industrial development and agricultural mechanization broke up traditional hacienda society, and millions of farm laborers were displaced from the land. In 1940 more than 65 percent of the Mexican workforce was engaged in agriculture, but that declined to less than 50 percent in 1970. In the meantime, more than 15 million new acres of irrigated land were put into production in the American Southwest, and along with industrialization, the need for unskilled laborers greatly increased. With wages in the United States three to four times higher than Mexican wages, millions of farm laborers crossed the border.

After 1945 changes in Mexican American society cleared the way for the more militant Chicano spirit of the 1960s. For decades the quest for Mexican American civil rights had been led by such groups as the League of United Latin American Citizens (LULAC) and the GI Forum, which worked in the courts, like the National Association for the Advancement of Colored People, to end *de jure* discrimination. By the late 1950s, however, Mexican American leaders realized that legal action was ineffective without political power, and in 1958 they formed the Mexican-American Political Association (MAPA) in California, the Political Association of Spanish-Speaking Organizations (PASO) in Texas, and the American Coordinating Council on Political Education (ACCPE) in Arizona. MAPA worked for only Mexican support whereas the others aimed for a coalition with White liberals, Black activists, and labor unions, but all three tried to mobilize Mexican American political power. John F. Kennedy's campaign in 1960 worked through MAPA, PASO, and ACCPE to form Viva Kennedy clubs, and in 1962 MAPA and PASO ran successful candidates in the Crystal City, Texas, elections. José Angel Gutiérrez rose out of those elections and in 1970 formed La Raza Unida, a political party dedicated to community control of Mexican American counties in south Texas.

Meanwhile, Corky Gonzalez founded the Crusade for Justice in 1965. Schooled in local politics and Denver antipoverty programs, Gonzalez demanded reform of the criminal justice system, an end to police brutality, and good housing, schools, and jobs for Mexican Americans. Culturally nationalistic, he also sponsored Chicanismo, a pride in being Mexican American. A host of Chicano writers and artists—including novelists Raymond Barrio and Richard Vásquez, short-story writer Daniel Garza, playwright Luís Valdez, and painter Raul Espinoza—evoked the Chicano spirit, and Chicano studies programs swept through the schools of the Southwest in the 1970s and 1980s.

Reies López Tijerina was another Mexican American activist of the 1960s and 1970s. A seminary-trained preacher who became interested in liberation theology, Tijerina traveled widely in Spain and the United States. In 1963, he formed the *Alianza Federal de Mercedes* (Federal Alliance of Land Grants) and demanded the return of land taken from *tejanos, californios,* and *nuevos mexicanos.* Militant and articulate, Tijerina was a charismatic leader who denounced racism and called for ethnic solidarity. In 1966, claiming millions of acres in New Mexico and urging secession, he "occupied" Kit Carson National Forest and assaulted several forest rangers. On June 5, 1967, Tijerina and his supporters raided the courthouse at Tierra Amarilla, New Mexico, shot two deputies, released eleven *Alianza* members, and fled the town with several hostages. Captured and sentenced to prison, Tijerina was paroled in 1971 on the condition that he dissociate himself from the *Alianza.* Without his leadership, the movement died.

The Brown Berets was founded in 1967 by David Sánchez in Los Angeles. Organized initially to protest political brutality, the Brown Berets started in group patrols to monitor police activities. They soon became more militant, wearing the distinctive brown berets, army fatigues, and boots to emphasize the self-defense nature of their ideology. The Brown Berets intended to defend the Hispanic community against Anglo violence. Although chapters of the Brown Berets were established throughout the urban Southwest, the group was strongest in California and Texas. In 1968, the Brown Berets organized a series of protests at high schools in California to demand improvements in public education for Hispanic children. Many of them were arrested and charged with a variety of narcotics, public order, and ideological crimes. They also engaged in several community service activities, among which the most important was the East Los Angeles Free Clinic, a medical facility funded by the Ford Foundation. In 1972, Sánchez led a Brown Beret "invasion" and "occupation" of Catalina Island off the southern coast of California, claiming that it was illegally taken from Mexican peoples.

No Mexican American leader rivaled César Chávez in influence. A counterpart in time and philosophy to Martin Luther King, he believed in nonviolence but put more emphsis on economic action than civil rights. In 1962, he organized the National Farm Workers (later the United Farm Workers), and the prevailing climate of opinion in the United States grew more favorable to the plight of farm workers. In 1960, Edward R. Murrow of CBS had broadcast Chávez's documentary *Harvest of Shame,* an exposé about the plight of migrant workers in the United States. One year later, Michael Harrington's book *Poverty in America* again brought the problem to public attention. Congress responded later in 1962 with the Migrant Health Act, federal legislation that funded private and public agencies to improve health care for migrant workers.

For three years Chávez built the union; then in 1965 he organized a strike against the Delano, California, grape growers, demanding better pay. The growers refused, and Chávez turned the strike into a moral crusade, an appeal to the conscience of America. The growers used violence, strikebreakers, and anti-Communist rhetoric; and Chávez appealed to White liberals like Robert Kennedy and Hubert Humphrey, labor unions like the AFL-CIO, Black leaders like Martin Luther King, and White students on college campuses. For five years Chávez led a national boycott of California grapes, fought the growers as well as the Teamsters Union (which tried to organize a rival union), and finally, in 1970, succeeded in winning a long-term contract with the growers. Chávez had been the most successful Chicano of all.

Many Puerto Ricans became similarly militant in face of the challenges facing them on the mainland. Especially troubling was their lack of a firm ethnic identity. Puerto Ricans received U.S. citizenship in 1917 and the right to elect their own governor in 1947, but Puerto

César Chávez, founder of the United Farm Workers of America.

Rican politics always revolved around the question of independence versus commonwealth status (granted in 1952) or statehood. Color also challenged Puerto Rican ethnicity. On the island, race had hardly been an issue; for centuries Whites, Blacks, mestizos, and mulattoes had mingled socially. But on the mainland a racial wedge split the community for the first time, with White Puerto Ricans aligning themselves with White Americans rather than with Black Puerto Ricans, and Black Puerto Ricans emphasizing their Spanish language to distinguish themselves from African Americans. In the 1960s, when the civil rights movement gained momentum, White Puerto Ricans could not sympathize with calls for integration and cared little about *de facto* segregation. Finally, most Puerto Ricans entered the cities just as job opportunities were shifting to the suburbs and employment required education and technical skills; they found only minimum-wage service jobs that would never lift them above the poverty line. Most Puerto Ricans joined the working poor—people with jobs that do not generate enough income for a minimum standard of living.

Not until the 1960s did Puerto Ricans begin organizing. Many joined the Democratic Party, and New York labor unions mounted campaigns to register Puerto Rican voters, but because of population dispersal and the Hispanic alienation from organizations, getting out the vote continued to be a major challenge. Some Puerto Rican groups concentrated on education. In 1961 the Puerto Rican Forum established Aspira to help young Puerto Ricans go to college. Aware that young people needed positive images, the Forum, Aspira, and the Conference on Puerto Rican Education became the most active groups in the Puerto Rican community. The Puerto Rican Legal Defense and Education Fund, a largely middle-class organization, promoted higher education and fought discrimination. Other Puerto Rican leaders promoted bilingualism and demanded bilingual teachers in schools, special programs to preserve the Spanish language, courses in Puerto Rican history and culture, and community participation in education. Arguing that the school system was top-heavy with Anglos and Jews, groups like the United Bronx Parents called for community control of schools, Puerto Rican administrators and teachers in predominantly Puerto Rican schools, and Puerto Rican paraprofessionals. Jewish and Anglo educators felt threatened, fearing for their jobs or lack of promotions in favor of Puerto Ricans, and decentralization met bitter opposition from the New York United Federation of Teachers.

Other Puerto Ricans opted for economic action. The Puerto Rican Merchants Association encouraged small businesses, and the Puerto Rican Civil Service Employees Association promoted the interests of Puerto Rican government workers. Under the War on Poverty program begun in 1965, the federal government funded a Puerto Rican Community Development Project that sponsored drug treatment, summer jobs, job training, and school tutoring programs. Puerto Rican workers joined labor unions and eventually constituted a major segment of the International Ladies Garment Workers Union. The East Harlem Tenants Council organized for lower rents, safer apartments, and better maintenance from landlords. Puerto Rican social workers formed the Puerto Rican Family Institute to assist families coming to the mainland, and after securing funds from the Council Against Poverty in 1965, the institute began marriage, employment, and family counseling.

Some Puerto Ricans turned militant. The Free Puerto Rico Now group and the National Committee for the Freedom of Puerto Rican Nationalist Prisoners advocated the use of violence to achieve Puerto Rican independence. During the 1960s the National Committee for Puerto Rican Civil Rights demonstrated for civil rights, affirmative action in the hiring of Puerto Rican teachers, police, and firefighters, and Puerto Rican studies programs in schools. The Young Lords, a militant group of Puerto Rican students formed in the 1960s, demanded Puerto Rican studies programs in the city colleges, community control of community institutions, and an end to police brutality.

Cuban Americans were just as militant, but the object of their wrath was not poverty and discrimination at home but Fidel Castro. In

1960 there were 124,416 people of Cuban descent living in the United States, but economic and political troubles in Cuba during the 1960s sent another 456,000 Cuban immigrants to the United States. In many ways they were a privileged group. Most were White, well educated, and blessed with important professional, technical, administrative, and entrepreneurial skills. Many possessed substantial capital resources and investment portfolios. They also arrived as political refugees, victims of a dictatorial Communist regime. When Cubans naturalized as U.S. citizens, most of them became conservative, anti-Communist Republicans, which provided the GOP new political opportunities in the once-solid South. The United States in the early to mid-1960s, before the Vietnam War changed the ideological landscape, was an intensely, even jingoistically patriotic society.

Cuban American militancy was channeled into anti-Castro activities. Cuban American politicians demanded that the federal government increase its political and economic pressure on Cuba until Fidel Castro was driven from power. Some Cuban American activists participated in paramilitary groups dedicated to Castro's demise. In 1961, more than 1,500 Cuban refugees joined Brigade 2506 and participated in the Central Intelligence Agency's botched invasion of Cuba at the Bay of Pigs. Although most of them were arrested by Cuban authorities, other Cuban Americans took up the mantle of militancy. Alpha 66 rejected all proposals for normalization of U.S. relations with Cuba, and Omega 7 called for the assassination of all Cuban diplomats at the United Nations. In 1983, Omega 7 activists bombed several Miami businesses whose owners wanted to do business in Cuba. Assassins from the Cuban Nationalist Movement killed Orlando Letelier, a former Chilean ambassador to the United Nations, because they considered him pro-Castro. In October 1971, José Elías de la Torriente of the group Cuban Forces of Liberation conducted a military raid on the small Cuban port city of Boca de Sama. In May 1972, thousands of Cuban Americans demonstrated in Washington, DC, chanting "Cuba must be free, and Cubans must free her." Other militant Cuban American groups included Comando Zero, Acción Cubana, and Bloque Revolucionario.

In the late 1960s and early 1970s, while Cuban Americans focused on international affairs and how they affected U.S.–Cuban relations, African Americans, Mexican Americans; and Puerto Rican Americans paid increasing attention to economic questions. "Freedom to go into a restaurant," argued Ralph Abernathy, who succeeded Martin Luther King as head of the Southern Christian Leadership Conference, "doesn't mean very much if you are too poor to order a meal. We must find a way for Black folk to climb the ladder to economic success in America." Until Blacks enjoyed the same economic and educational opportunities as Whites, they would always be second-class citizens in the United States.

Before his assassination, Martin Luther King had decided on a grand gesture to protest poverty in America—his famous Poor People's Campaign. He wanted to invite representatives of poor people from around the country to camp out at the Mall in Washington, DC, and express their concerns. When King was assassinated, leadership of the Poor People's Campaign fell to Ralph Abernathy. The Poor People's marchers arrived in Washington, DC, on May 11, 1968. Reies Tijerina and Corky Gonzales were among the Mexican American leaders, and representatives of Appalachian Whites, Hawaiians, Puerto Ricans, and various Native American peoples were also there. Thousands of marchers camped out on the grounds between the White House and the Capitol, constructing what came to be known as Resurrection City, a series of makeshift, temporary cardboard homes and tents. Abernathy demanded an end to the Vietnam War because it was diverting too much money from social programs and preventing the expansion of Lyndon B. Johnson's Great Society.

Although the Poor People's Campaign disbanded on June 23, 1968, participants left behind in Washington, DC, a new consciousness of poverty in America and how it affected minority groups. They also stimulated a new commitment to remedying the problem. One solution, of course, was expansion of federal government educational and job training programs. The other was the clarion call for "affirmative action," which would eventually polarize and racially politicize the civil rights debate in America.

Chapter Five

RED POWER

They appeared to be a group of tourists seeing the sights of San Francisco. Perhaps they had already ridden the cable cars, wandered around Fisherman's Wharf, walked up to Nob Hill, or negotiated their way down Lombard Street. It was November 9, 1969, and they crowded onto a chartered boat, ready for a cruise out to Alcatraz Island. Some looked like hippies or war-protesting college students, with long hair and military fatigues, but they were actually a group of radical Native American college students and urban Indians out to make a political statement. At first they were only going to circle Alcatraz and symbolically reclaim it for Indian people, from whom it had been stolen, they claimed. But the demonstration quickly escalated when Indian students from the University of California (UC) at Berkeley, UCLA, UC Santa Cruz, and San Francisco State University, along with other urban Native Americans from the Bay area, made their way by small boats out to Alcatraz and actually "occupied" the island.

A group known as Indians of All Tribes took responsibility for the occupation and issued a set of demands: that the federal government deed them a clear title to Alcatraz and establish there a university, museum, and cultural center dedicated to American Indians. They hauled radio equipment out to the island and began broadcasting "Radio Free Alcatraz" and published their own newsletter, *Rock Talk*. Journalists descended on San Francisco from all over the world, printing every word coming from the island. President Richard M. Nixon received thousands of telegrams, most of them sympathetic to the

Indian demands. One writer even noted, "For once in this country's history let the Indians have something. Let them have Alcatraz." As the occupation continued, representatives of indigenous peoples from Canada, South America, and reservations throughout the United States descended on Alcatraz to show their support.

Indians of All Tribes did not get title to Alcatraz, but the occupation lasted until June 11, 1971, and became an ensign to the Red Power movement—not only because of its dramatic militancy but because it represented the new power of urban Indian people and the pan-Indian spirit. Alcatraz inspired similar occupations throughout the country. In March 1970, a group known as United Indians of All Tribes invaded Fort Lawton, California, demanding its return to Indian people. Two months later, a band of Pomo Indians occupied Rattlesnake Island near Clear Lake, California, to establish an "ancestral claim" to the region. Later in the month, Mohawks occupied Loon Island in the St. Lawrence River. Pit River Indians tried to reclaim Lassen National Forest in June 1970, and in July, Oglala Sioux seized Sheep Mountain, North Dakota, which the U.S. government had taken as a military firing range. Acts of Native American protest spread across the country. In demanding self-determination, tribal autonomy, and respect for Indian cultures, Indians of All Tribes at Alcatraz set the stage for the Red Power movement: a series of powerful protests in the 1970s that empowered Indian people throughout the United States.

TERMINATION

Although Native Americans, like African Americans and Hispanics, adopted more militant tactics in the 1960s and 1970s, the nature of Indian militancy was fundamentally different, primarily because it involved so much more than the issues of individual civil rights and economic advancement. Some Native American activist groups pursued traditional civil rights issues. The Indian Rights Association and the National Congress of American Indians, for example, pushed the *Allen v. Merrill* case through the courts. The state of Utah had taken away the voting rights of Indians living on reservations, and the U.S. Supreme Court in 1957 declared the legislation unconstitutional. The National Indian Youth Council established the American Indian Movement for Equal Rights (AIMER), a civil rights advocacy group. AIMER campaigned to end voter discrimination against Indians, which still occurred in such states as Arizona and New Mexico, and employment discrimination. Another AIMER target was the Bureau of Indian Affairs (BIA), which had relatively few Indian people in management positions. Eventually, they wanted to create an all-Indian Bureau of Indian

Affairs completely separate from the federal government. During their most vocal period in the 1970s and early 1980s, AIMER members worked as watchdog groups in BIA offices trying to promote the hiring and advancement of American Indians.

But for the most part, Native American militancy transcended the traditional civil rights concerns of African Americans and Hispanics. At first, the Red Power movement focused on putting termination in a permanent grave. Activists were convinced that the key to the future of Indian peoples, especially those still living on reservations, was preservation of federal trust status, which insulated reservations from state and local legal jurisdiction and tax burdens. By destroying that trust status, termination would have done to all Indian peoples what it did to the Klamaths and Menominees—handed tens of millions of acres of Indian land over to Whites for commercial development. In the process, as the Indians lost their land, they would lose their culture as well.

President Dwight D. Eisenhower had stopped implementing termination in the mid-1950s, but the law remained on the books and hung over the Indians like a legal guillotine. Republican Richard Nixon won the presidential election of 1968, but he had trouble generating any enthusiasm among African Americans and Hispanics, who viewed the Republican Party as a group of elite, upper- and upper-middle-class Whites. In 1972, Nixon wanted to earn caché among minorities to strengthen his bid for reelection, and he felt most comfortable with Native American issues. In 1970, the president announced that the Bureau of Indian Affairs (BIA) had formally abandoned termination as federal public policy. "The special relationship between Indians and the federal government," Nixon said, "is the result of solemn obligations which have been entered into the United Sates government. To terminate this relationship would be no more appropriate than to terminate the citizenship rights of any other American." It was not until 1988, however, that Congress passed the Repeal of Termination Act, which prohibited Congress from ever terminating or transferring BIA services without the express permission of the involved tribes.

TREATY RIGHTS

The end of termination was Red Power's first victory, but it was hardly the last. By the time President Nixon announced the end of termination, the Red Power movement was in full gear, working at guaranteeing treaty rights, returning alienated land, protecting the environment, and self-determination. Controversies over treaty rights and treaty obligations galvanized Indian activists. In 1968, the Mohawks led the way. Under the provisions of Jay's Treaty, which the United States and Great Britain had signed in 1794, the Mohawk Indians of upstate New York had long enjoyed the right to cross the boundary between the United States and Canada in order to visit relatives among the Canadian Mohawks. The St. Lawrence River constituted the boundary between Canada and the United States, and the Cornwall Bridge across the river was the most frequently used crossing point. During the 1950s and 1960s, however, Canadian authorities began casually, and then systematically, inhibiting the movement of Mohawks back and forth across the border, which the Indians considered a violation of solemn treaty rights. In 1968, to protest the Canadian government's regulation of their movement, a number of Mohawk activists intentionally blockaded the bridge, disrupting traffic flow and creating one of the earliest acts of insurgency in the modern Red Power movement. Several Mohawks were arrested, but neither New York nor Canadian authorities were able to prosecute them. Mohawk and Canadian officials eventually negotiated a settlement that preserved Mohawk rights. In the wake of the incident, the Mohawks began publishing *Akwesasne Notes,* a journal that soon became the most widely recognized voice of Indian militancy.

Protection of treaty-based hunting and fishing rights attracted even more attention. Hunting and fishing rights possessed great symbolic value, because so many non-Indians in the United States viewed Indians as people still connected to the land, to a past when Americans of all races had fished and hunted to support themselves. It was common practice in the nineteenth century, when the federal government signed land purchase treaties with individual tribes, for Indians to retain hunting and fishing rights, much as the sellers of land could keep mineral rights.

By the 1960s, however, Native American hunting and fishing rights were under attack by state fish and game authorities, who wanted the Indians to be subject to the same regulations—hunting and fishing licenses, hunting and fishing seasons, and game limits—as non-Indians. Non-Indian commercial fishermen were particularly irritated that Native American commercial fishermen were not subject to the same regulations that, they claimed, allowed Indians to harvest more fish and sell them at a lower price. Under political pressure from non-Indian sportsmen and commercial fishermen, state legislatures passed laws subjecting Indians to the same regulations as Whites.

Many Native American activists staged "fish-ins" to protest the legislation. In Minnesota, Wisconsin, Washington, and Oregon, they defied state game laws, fished out of season, exceeded limits, and illegally harvested protected species. The activists were then arrested and spent time in jail rather than pay fines. A leading figure in the fish-in movement was Hank Adams, a Native American of Sioux and Assiniboine descent. Adams was born in 1947 on the Fort Peck Indian Reservation in Montana. A gifted athlete and student leader during high school, he moved to California after graduation and became involved in politics. Adams actively supported the John F. Kennedy administration, and in 1964 he refused induction into the U.S. Army until the federal government made good on all treaties with American Indians. That same year, as part of the National Indian Youth Council, he worked diligently planning actor Marlon Brando's protest march to the Washington State capitol in Olympia to demand preservation of Indian fishing rights. In April 1964, Adams went into the army. When he mustered out, he became director of the Survival of American Indians Association, a group dedicated to Native American fishing rights. In 1968, Adams focused his attention on the Nisqually River near Franks Landing, Washington, where he protested state attempts to limit Indian net fishing. He staged several fish-ins in Washington state, and in January 1971, he was shot and wounded on the shore of the Puyallup River near Tacoma, where he had intentionally set an illegal fish net.

The issue of Indian hunting and fishing rights made its way into the federal courts, where Indians argued that their treaty rights superceded state and local fish and game regulations. Several major court decisions upheld the Indian claim. For thousands of years, for example, various Native American peoples fished for salmon along the Columbia River. When White settlers began arriving in the Columbia River basin of what is today Washington and Oregon in the 1840s and 1850s, the tribes ceded land title to the federal government but negotiated treaties retaining their hunting, fishing, and meeting rights at "usual and accustomed places." But in the twentieth century, logging activities and river pollution began to compromise the salmon harvests. Even worse, construction of hydroelectric dams along the Columbia and Snake rivers inundated traditional fishing sites.

In the 1960s, to protect their fishing rights, a number of tribes sued in the federal courts. In 1969, one of those cases—*United States v. Oregon*—was decided by the Supreme Court. It ruled that Native American fishing rights did not come from Whites but had originated with Indian peoples. Treaties had guaranteed indigenous peoples the right to fish at their accustomed places and to enjoy jurisdictional control over their own fishing activities. The court also ordered that the federal government, state governments, and Indian tribes establish cooperative machinery to manage salmon resources. The decision led to the establishment of the Columbia River Inter-Tribal Fish Commission in 1977 to implement Native American jurisdictional authority and to coordinate fishing activities.

In 1974, Federal District Judge George Boldt presided over *United States v. Washington* and decided that the Pacific Northwest Indian tribes enjoyed the right to one-half of the annual off-reservation catch of salmon. Boldt also reserved to the tribes full authority to regulate tribal fishing on or off the reservation. Eventually, he also required Washington officials to work out a cooperative arrangement with the tribes to co-manage state fisheries and related environmental issues.

The federal courts similarly protected treaty-based hunting rights. Early in the 1970s, for example, state fish and game authorities in Washington tried to stop out-of-season deer hunting on the Colville Reservation. Back in 1891, however, the treaty between the federal government and the Colville tribe had specifically awarded the Indians year-round hunting rights. Although Washington state courts upheld the state's position, the U.S. Supreme Court, in *Antoine v. Washington* (1974), overturned it on the grounds that the Colville Indians enjoyed sovereign hunting rights.

The courts also made distinctions between Indian peoples who had formally renounced tribal membership and those who had not. Early in the 1970s, Oregon fish and game officials began arresting Klamath Indians who were hunting without state licenses and out of season on what had once been Klamath reservation land. When the Klamaths were terminated in the 1950s, the land had fallen into the hands of non-Indians. But the Klamaths sued, claiming that their hunting rights were protected by treaty, and the case of *Kimball v. Callahan* entered the federal court system, where the Indians' rights were upheld in 1974. Klamath Indians who had not voluntarily agreed to termination, the court ordered, retained hunting rights, whereas those who had voluntarily resigned tribal membership did not.

Subsequent federal court decisions have consistently upheld hunting and fishing rights. In 1991, for example, the case of *Lac Courte Orielles Band of Lake Superior Chippewa Indians et al v. State of Wisconsin* was decided. Wisconsin state fish and game officials had tried to impose restrictions on the length of the Chippewa spearfishing season, the number of lakes they could fish, and the size of their catches when they fished off of reservation land. The treaties that the Chippewas had signed with the federal government in 1837 and 1842 had granted them unrestricted fishing rights on and off the reservation. A federal district court agreed with the tribe, holding that Chippewa treaties guaranteed such fishing rights unless the state could demonstrate compelling health or ecological reasons for establishing such restrictions.

NATURAL RESOURCES

The Red Power movement in the 1970s also became concerned with protecting tribal resources and the natural environment. The case of

Black Mesa in Arizona and New Mexico became a symbol of Native American environmentalism. Because Indian religion often revolved around the land and the environment, the Indians frequently viewed technological and economic development as sacrilegious. In 1970, the Peabody Coal Company began strip-mining land at Black Mesa, Arizona, a region considered holy to the Navajo and Hopi people. At Black Mesa, Hopi and Navajo religion, tribalism, individuality, and community fused together. Thomas Banyacya, a Hopi traditionalist, in a letter to President Richard Nixon, wrote,

> The white man, through his insensitivity to the way of Nature, has
> desecrated the face of Mother Earth. The white man's advanced
> technological capacity . . . [and] desire for material possessions
> and power ha[s] blinded him to the pain he has caused Mother Earth
> by his quest for what he calls natural resources. . . . Today the
> sacred lands where the Hopi live are being desecrated by men who
> seek coal and water from our soil that they may create power for the
> white man's cities. This must not be allowed to continue.

Indian environmentalists were especially concerned about the future of their ancient homeland in the high deserts. Desert environments are particularly fragile and very slow to recover from environmental damage. In 1969, with support from environmentalists, Navajo and Hopi leaders organized the Black Mesa Defense Fund to lobby for an end to strip-mining on reservation land. In 1972 representatives from the fund appeared before the United Nations Conference on the Human Environment, creating enormous publicity against the project and successfully stalling it.

At the same time, Native American activists wanted to make sure that non-Indian economic interests did not unfairly exploit reservation natural resources. The Yom Kippur War of 1973 between Israel and the Arab states prompted much of the concern because the Arab oil boycott had produced staggering increases in the price of oil. Between 1973 and 1979, the price of a barrel of oil skyrocketed from $3 to $34 a barrel, and natural gas and coal prices jumped as well. Many Indian tribes, however, were locked into long-term contracts with various oil and coal companies who mined and drilled on reservation land. Located on the reservations of various Indian tribes were up to 40 percent of all U.S. uranium, 33 percent of U.S. coal, and 5 percent of U.S. oil and natural gas reserves. In 1976, to make sure that Indian peoples received competitive prices for the sale of those resources, the leaders of twenty-five tribes established the Council of Energy Resource Tribes (CERT). Peter MacDonald of the Navajo nation was a leading figure in the organization. CERT was committed to maximizing tribal profits and to training tribal leaders in the efficient management of tribal natural resources.

CERT also lobbied for federal legislation to protect reservation natural resources. In 1982 Congress responded to CERT pressure with two pieces of legislation—the Federal Oil and Gas Royalty Management Act and the Indian Mineral Development Act. Both laws contained provisions for the renegotiation of long-term royalty contracts, the establishment of joint economic ventures between tribes and private mining companies, the use of revolving funds to strengthen reservation economic infrastructures, and the provision of job training programs to develop reservation professional expertise. The laws also amended federal environmental laws to give tribes clear control of resource use on their own lands.

The federal courts sided with increased tribal authority over reservation natural resources. In 1985, the Supreme Court decided the *Kerr-McGee Corp. v. Navajo Tribe* case. Tribal authorities had long held that Indian tribes should be able to tax the profits of non-Indian entities doing business on the reservation and resented having to secure the permission of the Department of the Interior before imposing value-added and property taxes. The Navajo tribal council had signed a lease contract allowing Kerr-McGee to extract reservation coal in return for a fixed royalty. But when the tribe then levied a tax on the coal, the company refused to pay and sued, arguing that the tax had not been part of the original contract. The Supreme Court held in favor of the Navajos. In the 1982 case of *Merrion v. Jicarilla Apache Tribe,* the Supreme Court once again upheld the right of an Indian tribe to receive royalties as a property owner and to levy taxes as a sovereign political entity.

COMPENSATION AND LAND RECOVERY

Another focus of the Red Power movement was righting the wrongs of the past, either by securing compensation for alienated Native American land or actually securing the return of the land. Despite the work of the Indian Claims Commission, most tribes continued to feel that the U.S. government had treated them with fraud and criminal negligence, taking their land in the eighteenth and nineteenth centuries under false pretenses, and activists demanded compensation.

Red Power activists achieved a number of major victories. In 1971, Congress passed the Alaska Native Claims Settlement Act to protect the interests of more than 50,000 Eskimo, Inuit, and other Indian peoples. The legislation also gave the federal government clear title to more than 40 million acres of Indian land, in return for which the native peoples received an immediate $462 million cash settlement and $500 million in future payments for mineral rights. A total of 4 million acres was set aside for Native American corporations in cities, cemeteries, historic sites, and game reserves. Alaskan natives were awarded shares in newly created regional economic corporations, and village political corporations were given control over surface rights to the land and the power to distribute government entitlement payments. The regional corporations exercised power over subsurface mineral rights, distributed dividend payments, and invested the rest of the proceeds. Critics like John Upickson of the Arctic Slope Native Association charged that the legislation would eventually destroy indigenous cultures because it alienated tens of millions of acres of land, surrendered hunting and fishing rights, and stimulated economic development of Alaska's interior.

In some cases, however, Native American activists wanted back their land, not just cash settlements. Such groups as the Indian Land Rights Association, the Alaska Federation of Natives, and the American Indian Civil Rights Council demanded the restoration of tribal lands, denouncing the idea of monetary compensation for the loss of the Indian estate. The Lakota Sioux, for example, wanted the Black Hills back, not U.S. government checks. In 1868, the Fort Laramie Treaty ended hostilities between the Lakota people and the U.S. government and delineated the boundaries for the Great Sioux Nation Reservation, a tract of land that would allegedly be free of White intrusion forever. Within months of the treaty signing, however, the discovery of gold in the Black Hills brought a flood of White miners. Eventually, the federal government confiscated 7.7 million acres of the reservation, without compensating the Indians.

For Lakotas, the Black Hills is sacred geography, "the Mother's heart and pulse" of their people. Lakota traditionalists considered restoration of the Black Hills essential to the survival of tribal identity. In 1923, the Sioux filed suit with the Court of Claims, arguing that their land had been taken in violation of the Fifth Amendment to the Constitution. The case remained in litigation in the Court of Claims, the federal courts, and the Indian Claims Commission for the next fifty-seven years. In 1979, the Court of Claims agreed that the U.S. government had violated the Fifth Amendment in taking Lakota land and awarded the Indians $17.5 million plus interest. One year later, in *United States v. Sioux Nation of Indians,* the U.S. Supreme Court held for the Indians, rejecting the government's appeal of the Court of Claims decision.

Lakota leaders, however, were not about to accept a cash settlement. They wanted restoration of the Black Hills, not a monetary payment. Each of the eight participating Sioux tribes—Oglala, Rosebud, Cheyenne River, Standing Rock, Lower Brule, Nebraska Santee, Montana Fort Peck, and South Dakota Crow Creek—formally rejected the cash settlement. In 1986, several members of Congress sponsored the Sioux Nation Black Hills Act, which would have restored more than 1.3 million acres to the Indians, but concerted opposition from the South Dakota delegation blocked passage. The controversy still rages on today.

The Taos Indians of New Mexico did manage to get back sacred tribal land. Blue Lake in northwest New Mexico is an ancient holy place to the Taos Indians. They view it as a religious shrine, the source of life, and a manifestation of the great spirit of the universe. Blue Lake, economically and spiritually, was the center of their lives. But in 1906, the federal government incorporated Blue Lake and the surrounding 48,000 acres into the Kit Carson National Forest. Later, the U.S. Forest Service opened the area to non-Indian hunters, fishermen, and campers. Taos Indian leaders began demanding return of the lake, and in 1965 the Indian Claims Commission offered the tribe $10 million and 3,000 acres near the lake. Paul Bernal, a Taos leader, rejected the offer, telling the Indian Claims Commission, "My people will not sell our Blue Lake that is our church, for $10 million, and accept three thousand acres, when we know that fifty thousand acres is ours. We cannot sell what is sacred. It is not ours to sell." Blue Lake became a symbol of Indian land claims and a rejection of the notion that cash settlements could make up for assaults on Indian culture. In 1970, President Nixon came to support the Taos claim, and Congress passed the Taos Blue Lake Act, returning the lake and 48,000 acres to the tribe. Nixon also saw to it that 21,000 acres were returned to the Yakiama Indians of Washington.

Congress did react to the demands of the Penobscot and Passamaquoddy peoples of Maine, who argued that the state of Massachusetts had seized tribal lands in violation of a 1794 treaty. President Jimmy Carter wanted the dispute settled, and in 1980 Congress passed the Maine Indian Claims Settlement Act, which appropriated $81.5 million for the federal government to purchase 300,000 acres of state land for the Indians. In return, the Penobscots and Passamaquoddies agreed to pay state income taxes, send serious criminals to state courts for prosecution, and follow state environmental and fish and game laws on the reservations. One Penobscot traditionalist labeled the law "a gross sellout of tribal sovereignty and an affront to self-determination," but most Maine Indians hailed the fact that hundreds of thousands of acres of land would be restored to them.

CIVIL RIGHTS AND TRIBAL SOVEREIGNTY

One of the Red Power movement's greatest challenges in the 1960s and 1970s was reconciling the competing demands of tribal sovereignty and individual civil rights. The African American and Hispanic civil rights movements had attacked the *de jure* discrimination imposed on people of color by local, state, and federal governments, but the Native American civil rights movement sometimes involved discriminatory actions by tribal governments. Two federal laws—the

Indian Civil Rights Act of 1968 and the American Indian Religious Freedom Act of 1978—revolved around the dilemma.

The Indian Civil Rights Act of 1968 limited tribal sovereignty. Back in 1896, in the *Talton v. Mayes* case, the Supreme Court had upheld the inherent right of tribes to govern themselves. Immune from state and local jurisdiction, many tribes erected their own tribal criminal justice systems, complete with tribal police, tribal courts, and tribal judges. The court stated unequivocally that tribal governments were also immune to some provisions of the Bill of Rights to the U.S. Constitution. Tribal governments, the court went on, enjoyed a sovereign status rooted in aboriginal independence. In the original case a Cherokee court had convicted Talton of murder, but he appealed, arguing that since tribal court had not impaneled a jury, his Sixth Amendment rights had been violated. The Supreme Court ruled that tribal governments were not subject to the due process clauses of the Fourth, Fifth, and Sixth Amendments to the U.S. Constitution.

But early in the 1960s, the federal courts became the scene of increasing numbers of lawsuits from individual Native Americans accusing tribal governments of abusive treatment and violations of civil rights. When the courts would not assist them, they demanded congressional legislation, and a number of members of Congress decided that the time had come to act. Congressional hearings opened in 1962 to determine whether "Indians needed some guaranteed form of civil rights against the actions of their own governments." Formal legislation, however, did not pass Congress until 1968 when the Indian Civil Rights Act was enacted and signed by President Lyndon B. Johnson. The law was passed to "ensure that the American Indian is afforded the broad Constitutional rights secured to other Americans . . . [in order to] protect individual Indians from arbitrary and unjust actions of tribal governments." It applied the Bill of Rights, with several exceptions, to the actions of tribal governments. Tribal governments were not subject to the Establishment Clause of the First Amendment and did not have to provide legal counsel (free of charge) to indigent defendants, trials by jury in civil cases, or grand jury indictments in criminal cases. The Indian Civil Rights Act did require, however, that tribal courts advise criminal defendants of their right to a trial by jury, prohibited trial judges from simultaneously serving as prosecutors, insisted that tribal criminal law be written in clear, simple language, and forced tribal courts to keep complete, accessible records of criminal proceedings.

The American Religious Freedom Act dealt with similar issues. In the past, tribal councils had often circumscribed religious practices on reservations. In 1954, six residents of the Jemez Pueblo in New Mexico, who were Protestants, sued when the tribal council proclaimed that Roman Catholicism was the official religion of the reservation and banned the construction of Protestant churches on tribal land. Nor could Protestants bury their dead in the tribal cemetery or hold Protestant services in their own homes. But the federal district court found against the Protestants, arguing that the demands of tribal sovereignty were more compelling than the right of individual Indians to religious freedom. Five years later, in the 1959 case of *Native American Church v. Navajo Tribal Council,* a similar decision was reached. The Native American Church sued when Navajo tribal leaders banned the use of peyote in religious ceremonies on the Navajo reservation. The Native American Church argued that the tribal council was violating their First Amendment right to freedom of religion. But the federal courts sided with the Navajo tribal council, arguing that it was not subject to the U.S. Bill of Rights because it was a sovereign political entity in its own right.

But individual Indians continued to raise the issue, accusing some tribal leaders of egregiously violating freedom of religion. It was a difficult issue for Congress, especially because some Indian activists considered tribal sovereignty to be at the heart of self-determination. But with the American Indian Religious Freedom Act of 1978, Congress acted. It ruled that all Americans, including Indians, enjoyed the protection of the First Amendment, and that neither local nor state nor federal nor tribal governments could violate that right. The American Indian Religious Freedom Act, because it was passed in the form of a joint resolution of Congress rather than a formal law, proved to be quite weak, but it did proclaim that individual religious civil rights superceded the demands of tribal sovereignty.

SELF-DETERMINATION

By the early 1970s, the Red Power movement had increasingly developed into a campaign for self-determination. Although *self-determination*'s exact meaning was imprecise, several controlling principles emerged during the debate. First, self-determination involved Indian control of the government agencies dealing most directly with them. Having non-Indians administer Indian health, education and economic programs was unacceptable to self-determinationists. Second, self-determination called for an end to assimilationist policies and a restoration of tribal values and culture. Allotment, citizenship, compensation, relocation, and termination had all worked for the annihilation of tribal cultures. Third, self-determinationists insisted on maintaining the trust status of the tribes with the federal government. Although many non-Indians saw self-determination and the continuance of the trust status as a contradictory combination of paternalism and independence, Native American activists were convinced that Indians needed the trust status to protect them from non-Indian majorities at the state and local level. Finally, self-determinationists hoped to bring about the economic development of reservation resources so that Indians could enjoy improving standards of living without compromising cultural integrity or tribal unity.

During the 1970s, as a result of Native American militancy and pressures from White constituents, politicians in Congress enacted a series of laws that gave Indians more control over their lives and became the heart and soul of the self-determination movement. The Indian Education Act of 1972 was first. In 1969 the Kennedy Report called for serious reforms in Indian education as a prerequisite to addressing the problem of Native American poverty, and Congress tried to implement many of its suggestions. The legislation mandated parental and tribal participation in all federal aid programs to public schools that enrolled Indian students; appropriated money to fund community-run schools; allocated money to state and local education agencies, colleges, universities, and tribes to develop new Indian history, culture, and bilingual curricula; funded tribal adult education programs; provided funds for teacher training in Bureau of Indian Affairs schools; and established an office of Indian education, staffed completely by American Indians, in the department of education. Herschel Sahmaunt, a Kiowa educator, hailed the legislation because it gave "Indian people in reservations, in rural settings, and in the cities control over their own education."

The Indian Finance Act of 1974 was another important item in the self-determination agenda. It appropriated new money for reservation economic development and individual entrepreneurship, established a loan guarantee and insurance fund to encourage new business, subsidized loans to reservations for businesses, and provided outright grants to new businesses. Many Indian traditionalists criticized the measure for providing a White solution to Indian problems, but the legislation did provide new opportunities to Indian entrepreneurs.

In 1975, Congress passed the Indian Self-Determination and Education Assistance Act, which pledged the federal government to "assuring Indian participation in the direction of educational as well as other Federal services to Indian communities so as to render such services more responsive to the needs and desires of the communities." The law permitted tribal governments to directly contract social welfare and educational services; provided grants to train tribal personnel in financial management, human resources management, and administrative science; constructed new health facilities for Indian people; placed Indians in charge of all of these programs; mandated that school districts receiving federal money for Indian students spend those funds only on Indian students; and required those school boards to establish an Indian Parents Committee as an advisory body for all decisions having an effect on Indian children.

Finally, Congress pleased self-determinationists by passing the Indian Child Welfare Act of 1978. In 1958, the Bureau of Indian Affairs had joined hands with the Child Welfare League of America to sponsor adoption programs for Indian children. The goal of the program was to get Indian children out of their own families, off the reservations, and into the homes of White adoptee parents who would raise and educate them. The goal, of course, was assimilation. Under the adoption program, Indian parental rights had been terminated—often without their full participation, understanding, or consent—and children were legally adopted by non-Indian families, usually through the sponsorship of Christian churches. More than 1,000 Indian children were adopted under the program.

But during the 1970s, Indian activists bitterly criticized the program, describing it as racist and contrary to the needs of Indian families. Congress responded in 1978 with the Indian Child Welfare Act, which made it very difficult for non-Indian families to adopt Indian children. The law gave tribal governments exclusive jurisdiction over Indian children living on the reservations, transferred child custody proceedings from state to tribal courts, permitted tribal governments to intervene in child custody disputes, and required state social service agencies to comply with tribal wishes in the custody placement of all Indian children.

In 1989 the Supreme Court rendered its decision in *Mississippi Band of Choctaw Indians v. Holyfield et al.* The case revolved around two Choctaw Indian children born off the reservation in 1985 to unmarried parents who were members of the Mississippi Choctaw tribe. Both parents signed consent forms allowing Mississippi social services to place the children with a non-Indian family. The final adoption decree was issued in January 1986. In March 1986, the tribe asked for the decree to be vacated since under the provisions of the Indian Child Welfare Act of 1978, only the tribe had jurisdiction. The case made its way to the Supreme Court, which found in favor of the tribe, arguing that "Congress enacted the Indian Child Welfare Act because of concerns going beyond the wishes of individual parents, finding that the removal of Indian children from their cultural setting seriously impacts on long-term tribal survival and has a damaging social and psychological impact on many individual Indian children."

THE AMERICAN INDIAN MOVEMENT

No group played a greater or more controversial role in Native American activism during the 1960s and 1970s than the American Indian Movement. The American Indian Movement (AIM) had been established in Minneapolis, Minnesota, in 1968 by a group of Anishinabes (Chippewas) protesting police brutality. Among its founders were Dennis Banks, Mary Jane Williams, and George Mitchell. They used the Black Panthers as a model for their organization. In urban areas of the United States, where police forces were composed overwhelmingly of Whites who lived in the suburbs, relationships between the police and minority communities were usually tense and hostile. Indian people, AIM leaders claimed, were often harassed and beaten by police. AIM also wanted to lobby for improved city services for urban Indians. In one of their first acts, they established an Indian patrol to monitor police activities.

Using insurgent political tactics, AIM soon established chapters throughout most major American cities and participated in the 1969 occupation of Alcatraz Island by Indians of All Tribes. Russell Means, an Oglala Sioux raised in Oakland, California, became active in AIM in the early 1970s. On July 4, 1971, he led a protest at Mount Rushmore, and later in the year, on Thanksgiving Day, an AIM group occupied Plymouth Rock in Massachusetts and painted it red in symbolic protest. In February 1972, Means led a caravan of more than 1,000 Indians into Gordon, Nebraska, to protest the murder of Raymond Yellowthunder, an Oglala, and the community's refusal to indict the killers. The protest succeeded in securing the indictments and eventual convictions of the White men involved in the crime.

AIM leaders actively participated in fish-ins in the Pacific Northwest to protest state fish and game laws; and in 1972 they organized the Trail of Broken Treaties caravan to Washington, DC. Their demands in this protest included complete revival of tribal sovereignty by the repeal of the 1871 ban on future treaties, restoration of treaty-making status to individual tribes, the provision of full government services to unrecognized eastern tribes, a review of all past treaty violations, restitution for those violations, and the elimination of all state court jurisdiction over American Indians. They also invaded and trashed the offices of the Bureau of Indian Affairs in Washington, DC, to dramatize their demands.

In 1973, AIM orchestrated the seventy-one-day occupation of Wounded Knee, South Dakota. Several hundred AIM members had traveled to Rapid City, South Dakota, to protest the murder of Wesley Bad Heart Bull, an Oglala. Darold Schmitz, a White man, was charged with manslaughter in the case, but AIM protestors demanded an indictment of first-degree murder. On February 6, 1973, more than 200 AIM protestors fought with police in Custer, South Dakota, over the incident.

By that time, trouble had erupted as well at the Pine Ridge reservation. Oglala traditionalists resented the leadership of Richard Wilson, who headed the federally backed tribal government. When they protested his leadership, the government dispatched sixty federal marshals to Pine Ridge. The traditionalists asked AIM for support. AIM protestors arrived at Pine Ridge, and on February 28, 1973, an armed confrontation began in the village of Wounded Knee. The occupation began as a symbolic protest of Oglala Sioux politics, but once the FBI sent in 250 agents to surround the protestors, it became a broad-based protest of the plight of American Indians. The standoff lasted for seventy-one days, with AIM committed to the notion of tribal sovereignty and the federal government committed to the destruction of the American Indian Movement. The federal government then brought hundreds of charges against AIM leaders for their participation in the standoff, but of the 562 indictments, only fifteen convictions resulted, and these were for minor offenses. In the election for the tribal presidency of the Pine Ridge Reservation in 1974, AIM nominated Russell Means for the office. In the election, Wilson won by a narrow margin, and although the Civil Rights Commission recommended decertification of the election because of irregularities, the Bureau of Indian Affairs let it stand.

In 1975, AIM established a protest encampment at Jumping Bull near the Oglala village. Federal agents joined forces with the GOONS (Richard Wilson's Guardians of the Oglala Nation) and attacked the encampment. During the confrontation, a firefight took place. One AIM member and two federal agents were killed. Three AIM members—Bob Robideau, Darrel Butler, and Leonard Peltier—were brought to trial. Robideau and Butler were acquitted by an all-White jury, but Peltier was convicted of murder and given two life sentences.

To commemorate AIM's Trail of Broken Treaties march on Washington, DC, Dennis Banks sponsored the Longest Walk, which commenced in San Francisco in February 1978 and moved east across the country. Along the way, AIM members sponsored "teach-ins" and workshops to educate the public about Indian concerns. As the journey continued, other Indians joined in. On July 25, when they arrived at the Washington National Monument, more than 800 Indians were participating in the demonstration. There they issued a manifesto demanding civil rights for American Indians, tribal sovereignty, and the return of alienated lands.

By that time, however, the American Indian Movement was on the wane, as were most forms of civil rights activism. After Wounded Knee, AIM membership had gradually declined. AIM tended to be overrepresented by Sioux and Chippewas and failed to significantly broaden its tribal representation. The end of the Vietnam War took a great deal of steam out of protest movements in general, and the civil rights movement entered a long period of decline in the 1970s. With the passage of the Indian Self-Determination Act of 1975, many Indian peoples felt they had succeeded, at least temporarily, in reversing the direction of government Indian policy, and most Whites felt that the civil rights movement of the 1960s and 1970s had created a level playing field for all Americans.

Chapter Six

Affirmative Action, Busing, and the Disintegration of the Civil Rights Movement

As the school bus crested the hill and came into view, the mob tensed, and when the second bus was sighted, the shouting and screaming commenced. The crowd oozed hatred, and racial epithets peppered the air. "Get those niggers out of our schools," thousands chanted in unison, and rocks and bricks began to dent the buses and break windows. The Black children inside ducked for cover, brushing broken glass from their hair and clothes and praying for their lives. But this was not Little Rock, Arkansas, in 1957, or Anniston, Virginia, in 1961, or Oxford, Mississippi, in 1962. It was Boston, Massachusetts, on September 12, 1974, two decades after the *Brown v. Board of Education of Topeka, Kansas* decision and one full decade after the Civil Rights Act of 1964. The Black students were being bused from Roxbury High School to South Boston High School as part of a citywide desegregation plan, and White parents treated them like an invading army.

On June 21, 1974, Federal District Court Judge W. Arthur Garrity decided that Boston city school administrators had intentionally procrastinated implementing the Massachusetts State Board of Education's racial balancing plan, and he was tired of the excuses, the perseveration, the recalcitrance, and the obfuscation. Garrity took matters into his own hands and ordered that by the beginning of school in September, Boston would at least begin a busing program to desegregate the city's schools. The school board decided to proceed with what it called the South Boston-Roxbury High Paired School Complex desegregation plan.

The reaction in South Boston caught everybody off guard. Tucked into its own corner of the city, east of downtown, north of Roxbury, and surrounded by the Old Harbor, South Boston was composed largely of people of Polish and Irish descent, Roman Catholics who lived in working-class neighborhoods with a strong sense of community. In the early 1970s, hard times had come their way. The Yom Kippur War of 1973 and the Arab oil boycott of 1973–1974 had sent the U.S. economy into a tailspin, and the northeast especially suffered. Companies laid off large numbers of workers just when cold winter weather drove up the price of heating oil. Pummeled by unemployment and inflation, the people of South Boston were tense and edgy, worried about their futures, and the desegregation order brought out a latent racism. Black students had to run a gauntlet—from the school bus to South Boston High School's front door—of screaming, spitting White parents and children. A White mob set fire to the Summer Street Bridge to South Boston to block the passage of cars and buses. In retaliation, Black mobs rioted in Roxbury, smashing car windows, breaking into stores, and assaulting White motorists. Black radical Angela Davis held a rally and condemned White racism, and Bill Owens, a Black leader in Roxbury, announced, "We're going to go to school in South Boston, work there and live there, and the people of South Boston better accept that." Fighting and vandalism became endemic.

White parents organized a boycott. They formed a group known as Restore Our Alienated Rights (ROAR), and one of its leaders, a White woman whose son had been stabbed by a black student, announced, "I never heard of Judge Garrity until he made his fateful decision. He seems to have more power than any dictator who ever crawled the face of the earth. . . . With our last breath, we say to you [Garrity]—NEVER!" Of 550 White students in the junior class who were supposed to attend Roxbury High School, only thirteen enrolled. The rest either quit school or enrolled in private schools. White student attendance at South Boston High was not much better. The chaos was unrelenting, and in December 1974 Judge Garrity placed the schools in federal receivership and took them over. The busing plan to desegregate Boston's schools continued, but so did a seething rage among many Whites, some of whom had once, through their union leaders, supported the civil rights movement. How times had changed.

AFFIRMATIVE ACTION

On September 24, 1965, President Lyndon B. Johnson inadvertently gave birth to the affirmative action crusade when he signed an executive order that required all federal contractors to use what he called "affirmative action" in ensuring that minority workers were hired in numbers consistent with their ratio in the population. In doing so, the president was responding to a deep concern among civil rights activists that the movement to end racial discrimination had stalled. With the Civil Rights Act of 1964, most forms of formal, legal discrimination had been outlawed, but civil rights activists realized that a host of other practices and traditions, such as aptitude tests and union seniority rules, continued to militate against the hiring and promotion of minority workers and served to keep Blacks and Hispanics mired in poverty. Critics called these practices "institutional racism." Since Johnson's 1965 executive order, affirmative action has referred to a series of rules and regulations designed to counteract institutional racism and the effects of historical discrimination against certain designated minority groups.

Affirmative action also received a boost from the strengthening of the Equal Employment Opportunity Commission (EEOC), which had been created on July 2, 1965, as directed by Title VII of the Civil Rights Act of 1964. Its charge was to prohibit employment discrimination on the basis of race, color, religion, sex, or national origin. At first the EEOC's powers were limited to investigation and persuasion, but subsequent legislation greatly strengthened it. In 1972, Congress passed the Equal Employment Opportunity Act, which expanded the reach of Title VII to include state and local governments and educational institutions. Subsequent amendments to the law pushed the EEOC beyond persuasion and conciliation and empowered it to file suit against violators of the law. Although the original EEOC budget anticipated 2,000 cases a year, it investigated 49,000 cases in 1973, 71,000 in 1975, and more than 250,000 in 1980. Almost immediately, affirmative action had become central to EEOC culture.

Affirmative action also became central to the women's movement. The Civil Rights Act of 1964 had prohibited employment discrimination on the basis of sex, and women's rights advocates made affirmative action in hiring and promotion of women one of their major goals. By the early 1970s, affirmative action had become one of the primary policy goals of the National Organization for Women.

The idea of affirmative action was not without precedent in U.S. history. During the 1930s, when Commissioner of Indian Affairs John Collier launched the Indian New Deal, he implemented preferential hiring in the Bureau of Indian Affairs (BIA) for Native Americans. Section 12 of the Indian Reorganization Act of 1934 stipulated that BIA positions would go to Native Americans whenever possible, because only Indian people could really understand the dynamics and challenges of being an Indian in the United States. For the next several decades, such preferential hiring practices proceeded with little controversy.

But early in the 1970s, non-Indians challenged the practice, arguing that preferential hiring was a form of reverse discrimination against non-Indians and therefore violated the Fourteenth Amendment to the Constitution and the clause in the Equal Employment Opportunity Act of 1972 that prohibited racial discrimination. The protest of non-Indians became embodied in the case of *Morton v. Mancari,* which wound its way through the federal courts in the early 1970s. The U.S. Supreme Court heard the case in 1974 and upheld BIA hiring practices. The justices coyly avoided the race issue by arguing that being an "Indian" had little to do with skin color and everything to do with the existence of a "special relationship" between the individual and the federal government and whether the individual was defined as an Indian and covered by the federal government's trust obligation. Preferential hiring in the Bureau of Indian Affairs, therefore, was not racial discrimination as prohibited by the Fourteenth Amendment but simply an offer of special employment privileges to "members of quasi-sovereign tribal entities whose lives and activities are governed by the BIA in a unique fashion."

In their battle against institutional racism, affirmative action proponents first targeted intelligence tests, which they considered culturally biased against African Americans, Hispanics, and Native Americans. Many social scientists agreed that intelligence tests were racially and class biased in favor of the White middle and upper classes and against minorities and the poor. By relying too heavily on such intelligence tests, admission officers at elite universities and professional schools stacked the deck against minority applicants, and companies that used intelligence tests as an important criterion in job hiring and promotion decisions perpetuated the economic oppression of minorities.

Activists challenged use of such tests in *Griggs v. Duke Power Company.* The Duke Power Company required prospective employees to have a high school diploma and to achieve a certain minimum score on a general intelligence test as conditions of employment and promotion. The effect of the requirements was to exclude far more Blacks than Whites. In 1971, the Supreme Court rendered a decision in the *Duke Power* case, unanimously ruling against the company. Diplomas and minimum scores on intelligence tests could only be justified, and therefore constitutional, the justices ruled, if the company could demonstrate their direct relevance to the skills required on the job.

The use of intelligence tests, however, was not banned outright, especially when included as part of a battery of evaluative criteria, such as formal education, work and life experience, personal skills, and job interviews. In 1976, the U.S. Supreme Court decided the *Washington v. Davis* case, which revolved around the validity of intelligence tests. By a seven to two majority, the justices ruled that job qualification examinations were not inherently unconstitutional just because the test outcomes had racial implications. That Blacks performed more poorly than Whites was not *prima facie* evidence of bias and racial discrimination. "Disproportionate impact," the justices ruled, "is not irrelevant, but it is not the sole touchstone of an invidious racial discrimination forbidden by the Constitution."

Still, civil rights groups like the Southern Christian Leadership Conference, the National Association for the Advancement of Colored People, the National Urban League, the League of United Latin American Citizens, and United Native Americans campaigned for a ban on the use of intelligence tests in hiring. Ralph Abernathy of the Southern Christian Leadership Conference argued in 1973 that "intelligence tests are nothing more than a contemporary version of burning Ku Klux Klan crosses that intimidate and oppress black people." Many affirmative action programs in government agencies and private companies also worked to deemphasize testing.

In addition to condemning the use of intelligence tests in hiring and promotion practices, proponents of affirmative action attacked union seniority rules. Because minorities had often experienced discrimination in hiring and only recently had begun to enjoy relative equity in securing jobs, it had been impossible for them to accumulate seniority. But when the U.S. economy cratered in the 1970s because of rising energy prices and experienced high inflation and declines in production, manufacturing concerns began laying off many workers. The principle of seniority—"last hired, first fired"—was all but gospel in the labor union movement. For decades, labor unions had made hiring, promotion, and firing decisions based on seniority. The individual with the longest tenure of service enjoyed the most protection. Recently hired workers were the most vulnerable to layoffs. But civil rights activists argued that this policy primarily protected White workers and unfairly discriminated against minorities and that it would take decades before minority employees enjoyed the protections of seniority. They were not ready to defer equality for that long.

Early in the 1970s, a number of companies, to diversify their workforce and their management, began defying union seniority rules, retaining a certain percentage of minority workers during lean times and laying off more senior White employees and promoting minorities even when they did not have seniority. Many White workers with seniority found themselves being laid off or passed by for promotion when minority workers with less seniority succeeded. Claiming to be the victims of reverse discrimination, they filed lawsuits in the federal courts.

One of the most important cases was *United Steelworkers of America v. Weber,* which the U.S. Supreme Court decided in 1979.

The justices ruled by a five to two majority against the principle of seniority. Although Title VI of the Civil Rights Act of 1964 had prohibited racial discrimination in employment practices, neither the law nor the Constitution could prevent employers from adopting race-based affirmative action policies to promote minority workers to positions in which they traditionally had been underrepresented. Proponents of affirmative action hailed the decision, but most White labor union members considered *United Steelworkers of America v. Weber* a terrible setback for the labor movement and for the civil rights movement.

Affirmative action also addressed past discrimination against minorities in business. Throughout most of the twentieth century, federal government policies prohibited the awarding of government contracts to minority-owned businesses, especially in the South. A Black contractor, for example, was never allowed to bid for construction of a federal highway in Mississippi, nor could a Mexican American contractor expect to get a contract for an airport in Texas or Arizona. Such practices helped keep minorities from building successful businesses and entering the middle- and upper-middle classes. Because affirmative action programs were specifically designed to compensate for discrimination in the past, minority business owners began to demand special treatment from the federal government.

Their demands led to "minority set-asides." African American, Hispanic, Asian, and Native American business owners were classified as designated groups entitled to such set-asides. In a set-aside program, the federal government reserved a certain percentage of its contracts for minority-owned businesses, even if their bids were higher than some of those offered by White-owned businesses. Soon state, county, and municipal governments followed suit and established set-aside programs of their own. Most set-asides were used for government construction projects and procurement programs.

White business owners howled in protest. It was not at all uncommon for a White-owned business to submit the low bid for a proposed job, only to see the contract awarded to a minority-owned business submitting a higher bid. White business owners claimed reverse discrimination—arguing that the only reason they had been denied the contract was because of race—and logically claimed that taxpayers were paying higher prices for the job. Backers of minority set-asides countered with the argument that because minority-owned businesses had never been able to bid on such jobs in the past, their companies had not been able to grow substantially. Large, profitable, White-owned businesses, they claimed, could submit lower bids because they enjoyed economies of scale that smaller, minority-owned firms could not exploit. Without set-asides, minority-owned businesses would never be able to reach an economic level where they could compete with White businesses. In 1977 Congress passed the Public Works Employment Act, which stipulated a 10 percent set-aside for minority-owned businesses.

Opponents of set-asides sued in the federal courts, claiming that their Fifth Amendment rights to private property and due process and their Fourteenth Amendment protection against racial discrimination had been violated. The case of *Fullilove v. Klutznick* challenged the constitutionality of the Public Works Employment Act. In 1980 the U.S. Supreme Court heard the case and by a six to three vote upheld the constitutionality of set-asides designed to compensate for past discrimination against minority business owners.

Affirmative action also worked to increase minority representation in city councils, state legislatures, and Congress, but often the only way of increasing that representation was to redraw voting districts to create Black or Hispanic majorities. If all voting districts consisted of White majorities, so the logic went, minority candidates would be disadvantaged. Such logic offended many Whites, who insisted that they would vote for candidates based on political positions, not on race or ethnicity. But affirmative action backers insisted that race still played a huge role in American politics, and only by redrawing congressional, state legislature, and municipal district lines to create Black and Hispanic majorities would the number of minority officeholders rise.

Opponents sued, and the case of *United Jewish Organization of Williamsburgh v. Carey* tested the constitutionality of racially gerrymandering voter districts. In New York City, a redistribution measure enacted by the state legislature dramatically diluted the voting strength of the Hasidic Jewish community of Brooklyn and vastly increased the power of African Americans. The Hasidic community claimed that the redistricting had violated their voting rights. Improving the civil rights of one group, they argued, while reducing those of another group accomplishes nothing. The case reached the Supreme Court in 1977, and by a seven to one majority the justices found in favor of the state legislature. A state government does not violate voting rights, the court ordered, when it deliberately works to create Black or Hispanic electoral majorities.

Critics claimed that affirmative action had spun out of control—that what had begun as a well-meaning attempt to right wrongs in American society had rigidified in admission, hiring, and promotion quotas that amounted to little more than reverse discrimination against White males. The Fourteenth Amendment to the Constitution, they argued, guaranteed to every individual the right to equal protection under the law. Opponents of affirmative action even appealed to the words of the deceased Martin Luther King, Jr., who once said that he yearned for the day in America when every person would be judged "not by the color of his skin but by the content of his character." The chorus of protests from Whites became louder and louder, and the number of Whites filing reverse discrimination lawsuits with the EOC skyrocketed.

PLAYGROUND BATTLEFIELDS

But affirmative action was not the only controversial issue in the civil rights movement of the 1970s and early 1980s. School desegregation also raised tempers and generated consternation and hyperbole. Public schools had constituted the first theater of battle in the desegregation wars, and the NAACP's 1954 victory in the *Brown v. Board of Education of Topeka, Kansas* case launched the desegregation movement and precipitated the South's campaign of "massive resistance." By the 1970s, civil rights advocates had focused on poverty and *de facto* segregation as new fronts in the civil rights wars. Activists in the Hispanic and African American communities began to question the use of local property taxes to finance public schools. They argued that an individual right to an equal education was implied in the protections of the Constitution, the Bill of Rights, and the Fourteenth Amendment, but equal educations were not being delivered because of the way states financed public education. By using property taxes as the funding base, state and local governments guaranteed educational *inequality.* School districts with high property values automatically enjoyed abundant funds, whereas districts in economically disadvantaged areas faced tight budgets. The money spent per student in well-to-do areas was far higher than per-capita spending in poor districts.

Such disparities, civil rights advocates claimed, constituted racial and ethnic discrimination and were, therefore, violations of the equal protection clause of the Fourteenth Amendment. A series of lawsuits entered the federal courts in the 1970s to change public school funding. In 1973, the U.S. Supreme Court heard the case of *San Antonio Independent School District v. Rodriguez.* By a narrow five to four majority, the justices decided that property taxes did not constitute an unconstitutional funding formula because the right to an equal education was not guaranteed in the Constitution or in the Bill of Rights or Fourteenth Amendment. On those grounds, the equal protection clause of the Fourteenth Amendment was not relevant. The use of property taxes to fund public education, the Supreme Court concluded, did not deny anyone the opportunity for an education.

"Bilingual education" became another civil rights buzzword in the 1970s. Many prominent civil rights activists claimed that one reason for the underperformance of minority children in the public schools was that their first language was not English. They found themselves being taught in a foreign language when they had not even learned to read or write in their own first language. Many specialists in linguistics agreed, arguing that minority children should be taught content courses—biology, chemistry, physics, history, political science, art, and music—in their native language and then gradually be transitioned to content courses in English once they had mastered it as a second language.

In the 1960s, the Miami-Dade County schools pioneered bilingual education for Cuban immigrant children, and the students experienced great success. What was unique, of course, about the Cuban immigrants was their highly educated, middle- and upper-class background. Miami-Dade County had little difficulty finding among the Cuban immigrants a large cohort of trained, bilingual schoolteachers. Cuban students were taught all of their subjects in Spanish and then learned English in a separate class. The Cuban American children also enjoyed the support at home of highly educated parents who worked closely with them and with the school district.

The success of bilingual education among Cuban immigrants inspired other minority activists in the Mexican, Puerto Rican, Asian, and Native American communities to demand bilingual education for their children as well. When they encountered opposition from local school districts, they filed lawsuits, and one case—*Lau v. Nichols*—made its way all the way to the Supreme Court. *Lau v. Nichols* was a class action suit filed by Chinese American students against the San Francisco Unified School District. Claiming that the lack of instruction in Mandarin and Cantonese prevented them from being treated equally under the law, they based their appeal on the Civil Rights Act of 1964, which stated, "No person in the United States shall, on the grounds of race, color or national origin, be excluded from participation in, or be denied the benefits of, or be subject to discrimination under any program or activity receiving Federal financial assistance." In 1974, the Supreme Court found for the Chinese students. For the first time in American history, the language rights of non-English-speaking citizens received recognition as a civil right. The federal government then used *Lau v. Nichols* to require public schools throughout the country to provide bilingual programs for their non-English-speaking students.

Opponents of bilingual education attacked *Lau v. Nichols.* Gregory Rundberg of the group English Only! English Now! said, "My grandparents immigrated from Germany and had to learn English as soon as they got here. In fact, every immigrant in American history has had to learn English. How stupid can we get to change that now." Less ideological critics worried that bilingual education would sag and break down under the weight of the great diversity of immigrants settling in the United States during the 1970s and 1980s. Having teachers equipped to teach content courses in Spanish was one thing, but trying to find teachers to do so in Vietnamese, Khmer, Armenian, Azerbaijani, Gujarati, Hindi, and other languages was quite another. Schools in Queens, New York, in the late 1980s, had students speaking nearly 100 different languages. Finding certified, bilingual teachers to staff bilingual classrooms became impossible.

But even more explosive politically was the civil rights movement's adoption of busing to bring about racially integrated schools, which became one of the most controversial and bitterly contested issues of the 1970s and early 1980s. The Supreme Court's 1954 decision in *Brown v. Board of Education* ordered the desegregation of the nation's public schools and inspired protest and concerted resistance throughout the South. But by the late 1960s and early 1970s, when many southern school districts began to desegregate, it was obvious to most observers that segregated public schools were still common in the United States—not because of *de jure* statutes or school district regulations but because of neighborhood segregation. *De facto* segregation was common everywhere because Blacks and Whites lived in segregated neighborhoods. In most instances, it was an economic rather than legal phenomenon, a consequence of the rise of White suburban neighborhoods and the White flight from urban centers after World War II. Poverty confined minorities to inner cities, and they could not afford better housing in other areas. And because of such practices as red-lining, residential covenants, and racism among bankers and real estate developers, many Blacks who could afford better housing found it difficult to secure mortgages. The consequences were segregated neighborhoods and, because school attendance was based on residence, segregated public schools.

To overcome the *de facto* segregation of public schools, civil rights advocates in the early 1970s began calling for the mandatory busing of children across school district lines. A percentage of inner-city children would be bused daily to predominantly White schools, and an equal number of White children would be bused to downtown schools. Congress did not legislate such policies, but federal courts began enforcing them. Bitter protest erupted immediately from parents who resented seeing their children being transported long distances from their neighborhoods. Many White parents did not want their children attending inner-city schools, which they considered poorly funded and inferior. They argued that busing destroyed the idea of the neighborhood school and was certain to remove parents from school-based activities. Busing was also harmful to children, they claimed, because it forced them to spend hours each day on a crowded school bus. Many racist Whites opposed busing because they did not want Black children attending their schools. The violent protests in South Boston in 1974 dramatically illustrated what millions of White parents felt.

Lawsuits flooded the federal court system. On April 20, 1971, the U.S. Supreme Court by unanimous vote decided the case of *Swann v. Charlotte-Mecklenburg County Board of Education.* More than 24,000 Black children in the Charlotte, North Carolina, school district attended all-Black schools, and a court-ordered desegregation plan required that 14,000 of them be bused outside their neighborhoods. To those parents claiming that busing was a violation of their civil rights, the court stated that busing, racial balance ratios, and gerrymandered school district lines were all constitutional methods of desegregating schools as long as they were interim, not permanent, arrangements. The court acknowledged that there could be circumstances involving children's health or time traveled per day on buses that could become constitutional issues, but it refused to establish any guidelines.

Because *de facto* segregation was not confined to the South, northern Whites also had to confront the issue. The Denver, Colorado, schools, although mostly segregated, had never been segregated by law. School district officials, however, had frequently gerrymandered school district lines and purchased construction sites for new schools with segregation in mind. The case of *Keyes v. Denver School District No. 1* shed light on the issue. The Supreme Court decided it in 1973 by a seven to one majority. School officials had to desegregate a school system when the segregation was a result of school board policies, whether or not those policies had the force of law. School officials did not have to desegregate a school system where neither the law nor school district policies had created the problem originally. Nevertheless, the burden of proof to demonstrate that such segregation had not been intentional rested on the school board. Because Denver could not prove its innocence, the city was subject to court-ordered desegregation. With the court's decision in the *Keyes* case, legal ground was broken for the imposition of court-ordered busing in the North.

But the federal courts also imposed some limits on busing. It was obvious to most observers that court-mandated busing programs accelerated White flight to the suburbs. Civil rights activists wanted the courts to address that problem by implementing multidistrict busing decrees that would take minority children out of downtown schools and bus them to suburban schools, and take White students from suburban schools and bus them to inner-city schools. Such a requirement, they concluded, would make it impossible for White parents to escape the reach of desegregation. Critics claimed that such massive programs would keep some children in school buses for several hours each day, remove parents from contact with their children's teachers, and make extracurricular programs difficult to manage. Senator John Stennis of Mississippi captured the sentiments of busing opponents when he said, "Is there no end to this foolishness? Are we going to end up forcing children into boarding schools so their parents have no influence at all over their families and their children's education? Such liberal social engineering will ruin this country."

Opponents of multidistrict busing turned to the federal courts. The case of *Milliken v. Bradley* reached the Supreme Court in 1974, and the justices overturned a federal district court's multidistrict busing decree. The district court claimed that because Detroit's schools were already overwhelmingly Black, any plan limited to the city would never achieve integration. So the district judge implemented a busing decree that included Detroit and fifty-three surrounding school districts. Such a decree, the Supreme Court claimed, would be legitimate only if all fifty-three of those school districts had a history of engaging in *de jure* (legal) segregation of their schools. Because many of them did not, the decree was unconstitutional.

Opposition to busing among Whites, particularly in the South and throughout the blue-collar neighborhoods of the Northeast and Midwest, weakened the Democratic Party and gave Republicans new opportunities. Richard M. Nixon first exploited this discontent in his 1968 presidential campaign. In the election of 1964, Republican Barry Goldwater had proved that a conservative Republican could do well in the deep South, and his success there had caught Democrats off guard. Ever since the Civil War they had come to rely upon the so-called solid South as a guaranteed set of electoral votes in presidential elections. The Kennedy and Johnson administrations, with their emphasis on civil rights, had offended many White southerners, who began to see in the Republican Party the best chance of preserving the status quo. When Nixon won the Republican presidential nomination in 1968, he decided to implement a "southern strategy" in order to win the election.

It was a tricky business. Nixon did not want to pander to southern conservatives and lose the support of more moderate Republicans in the Midwest, Northeast, and border states, where he needed significant support. It would have been easy for him to appeal to the South by denouncing the Civil Rights Act of 1964 and the Voting Rights Act of 1965, but he feared that condemning the legislation would cost him more votes in the North than it would gain him in the South. Nixon also realized that a good number of Republicans supported the recent civil rights legislation. He had to find a way to appeal to southerners without alienating mainstream Republicans.

Busing was the answer. Instead of publicly condemning civil rights legislation, Nixon proclaimed the virtues of law and order and denounced the busing of school children to achieve racial integration. Without even mentioning the civil rights movement, Nixon managed to endear himself to millions of southern Democrats and to substantial numbers of blue-collar northern Democrats. Privately, he also encouraged southern political leaders to believe that if he won the election, he would make sure that conservative southerners were appointed to the federal bench, including the U.S. Supreme Court. In both the elections of 1968 and 1972, Nixon swept the deep South, and subsequent Republican presidential candidates—including Ronald Reagan, George Bush, and George W. Bush—have perpetuated the southern strategy in their own election campaigns.

Opponents of busing tried repeatedly in the 1970s to secure legislation outlawing the practice, but in a Democratically controlled Congress, they had difficulty securing majority support. In 1980, however, Congressman James M. Collins of Texas and Senator Jesse Helms of North Carolina pushed through Congress a law that prohibited the Justice Department "from bringing any sort of action that would require, directly or indirectly," the busing of children beyond the confines of a neighborhood public school. President Jimmy Carter, however, vetoed the measure, and subsequent attempts to resurrect the measure failed.

Opponents of busing also tried to get Congress to pass a constitutional amendment to prohibit busing, but the proposals never secured sufficient support. Senator Sam Ervin of North Carolina said, "I favor statutes to put an end to this tyranny immediately, and a constitutional amendment to put an end to it forever. . . . I am reminded somewhat of a story about the man who was away from home and received a telegram from his undertaker saying, 'Your mother-in-law died today, shall we cremate or bury?' He wired back and said, 'Take no chances: Cremate and bury.' I would cremate first by legislation and then bury by constitutional amendment." But Senator Ervin did not get either, and busing remained the law of the land.

School busing and affirmative action drove a wedge into the original civil rights coalition and robbed it of much of its influence. During the late 1950s and early 1960s, the civil rights movement had coalesced around several prominent constituencies in the Democratic Party, including African Americans, Hispanics, Jews, intellectuals, blue-collar workers, and labor union officials. Because Blacks constituted only 12 percent of the American population, their chances of securing federal civil rights legislation depended largely on their ability to win the loyalty of large numbers of Whites. They managed to do so under the leadership of Martin Luther King, whose nonviolent civil disobedience did not seem so threatening and whose condemnation of legal segregation gave civil rights advocates the moral high ground. Fair-minded people of every ethnic group instinctively knew that keeping an individual from the right to vote, hold public office, or attend school on the basis of race was inherently wrong. The Constitution, most Americans agreed, was color-blind.

The Black Power movement and Black rioting in urban centers during the 1960s had bruised the civil rights coalition, but the advent of affirmative action and school busing mortally wounded it. Many Whites became convinced that the civil rights movement had gone too far—that what had once been a morally justifiable demand for constitutional rights had become a dangerous, convoluted experiment in social engineering and reverse discrimination. Senator William Roth, Republican of Delaware, captured the sentiments of most conservative Whites when he called affirmative action and busing symbols "of a massive reformist effort by the Federal courts . . . to integrate the schools by means of a socially disruptive, financially burdensome, and administratively unfeasible regime of race quotas. . . . Through the imposition of an ill-conceived theory of social justice, these judges . . . have distorted the spirit of democratic government to achieve an end mandated neither by logic [n]or constitutional guarantee."

Part

III
—

OLD WOUNDS, NEW INJURIES, 1981–2000

The rioting erupted spontaneously on November 22, 1987, in the federal detention centers in Oakdale, Louisiana, and Atlanta, Georgia, where several thousand Cuban immigrants were being held. They took correctional officers hostage; set fires to mattresses, tables, chairs, and anything else that would burn; broke windows and smashed radios, television sets, and video cameras; and then demanded their rights under the U.S. Constitution and protections against unlawful incarceration. The standoff lasted for two weeks and ended only when Agustín Román, the auxiliary Roman Catholic bishop of Miami, intervened and negotiated the release of the hostages and an end to the rioting.

Until 1980, most Cuban immigrants to the United States had come from highly educated, middle- and upper-class business and professional backgrounds or from small-business entrepreneurial groups. Because they came from the more well-to-do classes in Cuban society, there were relatively few Afro-Cubans among them. Most Americans came to perceive the Cuban immigrants as political refugees from a Communist dictatorship who had earned reputations as politically conservative, hard-working, and law-abiding people.

But the so-called Mariel boatlift, which began in 1980 and eventually brought more than 125,000 new Cuban immigrants to the United States, changed those perceptions. On April 21, 1980, Fidel Castro announced that any Cubans wanting to go to the United States could leave Cuba through the port of Mariel. In a matter of hours, hundreds of Cuban Americans in motorboats left Miami and crossed the Florida Straits to pick up relatives at Mariel. Tens of thousands of Cubans crowded into Mariel, hoping to hitchhike a ride to America. Between April 21 and September 26, 124,779 Cubans left the island in what journalists dubbed the "Freedom flotilla" or the "Mariel boatlift." But before Cuban Americans were allowed to rescue their relatives, Castro also insisted that they agree to take strangers as well, and Castro selected the strangers: prostitutes, homosexuals, the criminally insane, the mentally retarded, and mental hospital patients. To be sure, the strangers were only a tiny minority of the so-called Marielitos, but the American press made the most of the story. Too many Americans concluded that all of the Mariel immigrants were tainted social misfits, that Castro had emptied the jails and asylums of Cuba.

The rumors did contain a grain of truth. Approximately 26,000 of the Marielitos did have prison records, but most had been jailed for anti-Castro activities, stealing food, or trading on the black market. Nearly 5,000 possessed recidivist criminal records, and several thousand more did have histories of mental illness. All told, perhaps 6 percent of the Marielitos came to the United States with serious problems. But only 350 had committed serious felony crimes in Cuba, and only 300 had been hospitalized for chronic mental problems. Between 1980 and 1987, the Marielito immigrants committed 2,800 crimes after arriving in the United States, of which only 600 were serious felonies, a number not much higher than the national average. The convicted Cuban felons were doing time in federal and state prisons.

Nevertheless, the Justice Department and the Immigration and Naturalization Service began detaining other Mariel immigrants deemed a threat to law and order but who had not committed crimes. By 1982 nearly 3,000 of them had been imprisoned at Oakdale, Louisiana, and Atlanta, Georgia, where they were held while the State Department negotiated a deportation agreement with Cuba. On December 14, 1984, Cuba and the United States signed an agreement providing for the repatriation of the detainees. The agreement called for the deportation of 2,746 "excludable aliens" being held in the detention centers, and future negotiations would take place to arrange for the deportation of the other convicted Cuban felons. In February 1985 the first contingent of forty detainees arrived in Cuba.

The negotiations broke down in May 1985 when the U.S. Information Agency established Radio Martí in Florida and began broadcasting anti-Castro programs into Cuba. An enraged Fidel Castro suspended the deportation agreement, and the detainees continued to languish in prison cells in Oakdale and Atlanta. Negotiations soon resumed, and on November 21, 1987, a new deportation agreement was reached in which Cuba agreed to take back the detainees, and the United States agreed to receive 27,000 Cuban immigrants annually. By that time, many of the detainees, who had spent years in prison without ever having been convicted of a crime, just wanted out, and they did not want to go back to Cuba. Their pent up frustrations exploded into the prison riots of late November and early December of 1987. Early in 1988, after the intervention of Bishop Agustín Román, the rioting ended, and the Immigration and Naturalization Service gradually began releasing some of the detainees to their families in the United States, whereas those with serious criminal records or mental health problems were returned to Cuba.

The Mariel boatlift and the prison riots of 1987 highlighted for most Americans the changing pattern of Cuban immigration, but it also symbolized changing patterns of immigration in general. During the seventeenth, eighteenth, and early nineteenth centuries, the vast majority of immigrants to America had been from northern and western Europe—particularly the British Isles, Germany, and Scandinavia. Late in the nineteenth and early in the twentieth centuries, a shift occurred. The flow of immigrants from northern and western Europe slowed to a trickle, and a flood of immigrants from southern and eastern Europe began. Italians, Greeks, Poles, Lithuanians, Russians, Czechs, Slovaks, Serbs, Croatians, Slovenians, and Hungarians soon dwarfed the numbers of British, German, and Scandinavian immigrants. Immigration demographics changed again in the 1970s and 1980s. The Immigration and Nationality Act of 1965 had scuttled the old quota system, and prospective immigrants from all over the world now enjoyed an equal opportunity to immigrate to the United States. And they did. European immigrants were swamped in numbers by immigrants from Mexico, Central America, the Caribbean, Southeast Asia, South Asia, and East Asia, and the ethnic profile of the United States became more complicated than ever.

Chapter Seven

THE NEW IMMIGRANTS

The case had all the makings of a spy thriller, a conspiracy of espionage unprecedented since the 1950s, when Congressman Richard Nixon accused Alger Hiss of handing over classified information to the Soviet Union and Julius and Ethel Rosenberg were executed for giving the Russians the secret to the atomic bomb. Later, newspapers, magazines, and television broadcasts crackled in 1999 and 2000 with the news that a Red Chinese conspiracy had compromised the nuclear weapons laboratories at Los Alamos, New Mexico. The Federal Bureau of Investigation moved in on the case, and agents swarmed over New Mexico. The Central Intelligence Agency tried to assess the damage overseas. The FBI arrested Wen Ho Lee, a Chinese American physicist working at Los Alamos and charged him with fifty-nine counts of espionage, enough to earn a death sentence or at least life in a federal prison. Lee's supposed threat to national security was so great that he was held without bail and in solitary confinement for nine months while the investigation continued. The press had a field day with Lee and all but demonized him.

But Lee's professional colleagues and neighbors in the close-knit Los Alamos scientific community backed their friend and concluded that the FBI, desperate to close the case and explain how U.S. nuclear secrets had made their way to Beijing, was engaging in a witch hunt and that Lee was being targeted primarily because he was of Chinese ethnic descent. They began raising money for his legal defense and hiring top-quality legal talent. The FBI's investigation did prove that Lee had downloaded material on thermonuclear warheads to a personal computer, but it was soon learned that many other scientists often did the same thing in order to work at home. The FBI's case against Lee slowly began to unravel. FBI agents began offering plea bargains trying to get Lee to plead guilty to a variety of lesser felony offenses, but he refused, insisting on his innocence. In the end, the FBI's case collapsed, and Lee pled guilty to a single misdemeanor offense of mishandling government documents. He was sentenced to time served. "This investigation," wrote a federal prosecutor who later looked into the Lee case, "was a paradigm of how not to manage and work an important counter-intelligence case."

The Asian American community rallied to Lee's defense, accusing the FBI of conducting an egregious case of racial profiling and a gross violation of Lee's civil rights. A letter writer to *Time* magazine in October 2000 noted concerning the case, "Deeply rooted anti-foreigner sentiment triggered a witch hunt that hurt Chinese Americans and tarnished the image of the U.S. Selfish politicians exploited the fictitious 'Chinese threat' for their own political gain, while a prejudiced law-enforcement agency abused the constitutional rights of someone yet to be convicted by a court. Much more work is ahead before Chinese Americans gain a voice in the American political scene as African Americans have done."

AFRO-CARIBBEANS

Political and economic instability in the Caribbean prompted the immigration to the United States of millions of people of African descent. Between 1890 and 1930, approximately 350,000 Blacks left the islands of the British West Indies—Barbados, Bermuda, Jamaica, Trinidad, Tobago, the Bahamas, the Turks and Caicos, Antigua, Barbuda, Redonda, St. Kitts, the Virgin Islands, Dominica, Grenada, Nevis, St. Lucia, St. Vincent, and the Grenadines—for the cities of the Northeast, especially New York City. Although they faced the same racial prejudice African American migrants from the South encountered, they were culturally different. They spoke standard English, worshiped as Roman Catholics or Episcopalians, placed great value on education, and nursed middle-class values. They became prominent in the needle trades, participated in the clothing workers' unions, and dominated the cigar-making industry. Blessed with strong entrepreneurial instincts, they maintained family-based rotating credit associations, known as *ensusus,* to finance one another's small businesses, and by the time of World War II, most of New York City's Black professionals and business owners claimed a West Indian ancestry. After World War II, the migration continued, with 60,000 British West Indians arriving in the 1950s, 105,000 in the 1960s, 225,000 in the 1970s, 240,000 in the 1980s, and 255,000 in the 1990s. Like their predecessors, most of them settled in New York City and across the Hudson River in northern New Jersey.

In the 1990s, many Whites and Blacks in the United States began to wonder why the British West Indians and their descendants—from Malcolm X to Secretary of State Colin Powell—enjoyed greater chances for success in the United States than African Americans whose ancestors had lived in the southern states. Although both groups had originated in West Africa and encountered similar racial prejudice in America, those of British West Indian descent were ten more times likely than southern Blacks living in New York City to start successful businesses and earn professional degrees. Their average family incomes were triple those of southern Blacks.

Most immigration historians had an explanation. The British West Indies had for the most part been all-Black societies, even during the days of slavery, with absentee landlords using Black overseers to manage their businesses in the Caribbean. Unlike southern Blacks, who were always outnumbered by Whites, West Indian Blacks did not grow up worrying about the everyday whims of White people. As a result, they developed a culture of independence. Also, Great Britain abolished slavery in 1830 and then instituted decent public schools in the islands, whereas southern Blacks suffered poor school systems well into the 1970s. Although slavery was abolished in the United States in 1865, Blacks had to endure another century of oppression and segregation. When West Indian Blacks began immigrating to the United States, they were well-educated, English-speaking people accustomed to making their own decisions. Not surprisingly, they were far more prepared for success in the United States than their counterparts from the southern states.

The Dominican Republic also sent hundreds of thousands of immigrants of African descent to the United States. The Dominican Republic covered the eastern two-thirds of the island of Hispaniola in the Caribbean. During the 1960s more than 100,000 Spanish-speaking Dominicans, most of them of African or mixed African Spanish ancestry, settled in the United States, primarily in New York City and especially in upper Manhattan and in the Corona-Jackson Heights neighborhoods of Queens. The migration accelerated during the 1970s, with 150,000 Dominicans arriving in the United States. That number jumped to 210,000 people in the 1980s and 240,000 in the 1990s. By 2000 there were nearly 600,000 people of Dominican descent living in the United States, approximately 15 percent of the population of the Dominican Republic.

Like the first wave of Cuban immigrants and Blacks from the British West Indies, the Dominicans were unusually prepared for economic success. Most came from the Cibao region of the Dominican Republic, where middle-class values were entrenched and family incomes and education well above the national average. Dominicans placed great value on stable, two-parent families, and many of the immigrants took jobs in service industries or started small businesses. By 1990, the family incomes of Dominican Republic immigrants exceeded those of Puerto Ricans living in the United States.

Although a few thousand Haitians immigrated to the United States during the nineteenth and early twentieth centuries, the great migration of Haitians was a phenomenon of the post-World War II era, particularly after 1957 when François Duvalier came to power and ruled with an iron hand. Almost as soon as Duvalier began exercising power, an exodus of urban professionals and small business entrepreneurs began, most of them ending up in New York City. Smaller Haitian communities soon appeared in Philadelphia, Boston, Washington, DC, and Miami. Duvalier's son—Jean-Claude Duvalier—only made matters worse, proclaiming himself "president for life" and sending the economy into a tailspin, making Haiti the poorest country in the western hemisphere. By the early 1970s, the Haitian immigrants consisted largely of the urban and rural poor. More than 250,000 Haitians settled in the United States after 1960, and by 2000 the immigrants and their children and grandchildren numbered more than 1 million people. Miami and New York City eventually became the centers of Haitian immigrant culture in the United States.

Haitians faced unique challenges in the United States. Because they were overwhelmingly of African descent, they encountered the same racism so many other immigrants from Africa and the Caribbean faced, but because they spoke French, not Spanish, they had difficulty making common cause with Cubans, Dominicans, and Puerto Ricans. And although the vast majority of Haitians are Roman Catholics, they practice a syncretic religion retaining elements of African voodoo. To the Irish and French priests serving in Haiti, the peasant religion— with the drinking of bull and chicken blood at religious ceremonies, ritual mud baths, hexes and charms, and identification of St. Jacques with the African god of war *Ougou Feray*—epitomized sacrilege. Finally, many African Americans resented the Haitian immigrants, whom they saw as competition for scarce jobs.

The resentment of the Haitian immigrants mounted to such a level that in 1978 the Jimmy Carter administration stopped acknowledging Haitian immigrants as political refugees, which made it very difficult for them to secure resident visas in the United States. The practice continued in the Ronald Reagan and George Bush administrations, even though the Refugee Act of 1980 defined a refugee as anyone possessing a well-founded fear of discrimination on the basis of race, religion, nationality, or politics. The Immigration and Naturalization Service (INS) characterized the Haitian immigrants as desperate people escaping the poverty of their homeland, a condition that does not qualify them for permanent status.

Unable to immigrate legally, desperate Haitians by the tens of thousands took to small boats and rafts and tried to float the 800 miles from Haiti to Florida. They assumed that if they could just get to the United States, their chances of securing permanent visas would improve dramatically. The U.S. Coast Guard intercepted thousands of them on the high seas before they ever reached American shores and took them back to Port-au-Prince, and an estimated 50,000 Haitians died at sea. The INS then launched deportation proceedings, but before the immigrants could ever be sent home, they usually melted into the Haitian communities of Miami and New York City and disappeared. Civil liberties groups protested that illegal Haitian immigrants were being treated differently under the law than Cuban immigrants. In 1986 the Immigration Reform and Control Act awarded resident alien status to all undocumented residents who could prove they had lived in the United States since 1982.

Haitian immigration became a political issue in the presidential election of 1992. In 1990, Haitians had elected Jean-Bertrand Aristide as president, but a military coup toppled him in 1991. Tens of thousands of Haitians constructed makeshift boats and rafts and set out on the high seas for America. The Bush administration had U.S. Coast Guard vessels intercept as many as possible, but during the election campaign, Democratic candidate Bill Clinton promised to evaluate each Haitian's refugee status after his or her arrival in the United States. When Clinton won the election, literally hundreds of thousands of Haitians began constructing boats and setting sail. The INS ruled that most of them were fleeing poverty, not political oppression, and refused to give them asylum. The Haitian immigrants had few supporters in the United States, and President Clinton decided to pursue the Reagan-Bush strategy of intercepting them before their arrival. Eventually, President Clinton had to deploy U.S. troops to Haiti and supervise the island's return to democracy to stem the immigrant tide.

THE HISPANIC KALEIDOSCOPE

Hispanic America was becoming more diverse as well. Cubans, Mexicans, and Puerto Ricans had for decades constituted the backbone of the Hispanic community in the United States, and their numbers continued to increase during the 1970s, 1980s, and 1990s. The Mariel boatlift of 1980 and 1981 had brought more than 100,000 Cuban immigrants to the United States, and another 150,000 Cubans immigrated during the rest of the decade. In the 1990s, nearly 220,000 Cubans crossed the Florida straits for a new life in America, with most of them ending up in South Florida. The numbers of Cuban immigrants increased so dramatically, and their socioeconomic background changed so much—with greater numbers of poor, less-educated workers among them—that some politicians considered legislation placing limits on immigration from the island. But because Fidel Castro maintained an iron grip on Cuba, the immigrants could claim to be political refugees and secure permanent resident visas anyway.

Puerto Ricans continued to settle in the United States as well. As U.S. citizens, they were free to settle anywhere in the country. Limits could not be placed on their relocation. New York City acted like a magnet to Puerto Ricans, especially the Bronx, the South Bronx, the Lower East Side of Manhattan, Spanish Harlem, and the Williamsburgh section of Brooklyn. In 1960, the number of Puerto Ricans in the United States totaled 900,000 people. That number jumped to 1.4 million in 1970, 1.7 million in 1980, 2.2 million in 1990, and approximately 2.6 million in 2000.

Although the Immigration and Nationality Act of 1965 had imposed limits on immigration from Mexico, illegal immigration continued unabated. Mexican population growth, at 3.5 percent annually, added 2 million people to the workforce each year, but the economy could not absorb them. At the same time, because of agricultural mechanization in Mexico, millions of farm laborers had been displaced from large commercial haciendas. In the 1980s, the unemployment rate in Mexico averaged 30 percent, and it declined only modestly from there in the 1990s. With jobs more abundant in the United States and wage levels three to four times higher, Mexican workers headed north in droves. Between 1945 and 2000, U.S. border patrols captured more than 25 million undocumented Mexican aliens trying to get into the United States. Many of them, as soon as they were deported to Mexico, tried again and again until they finally succeeded. By the year 2000, the number of people of Mexican descent—U.S. citizens, resident aliens, and undocumented, illegal immigrants—exceeded 20 million.

During the 1970s and early 1980s, when the U.S. economy experienced both inflation and unemployment, the arrival of so many undocumented Mexican immigrants raised the ire of labor unions and blue-collar workers, who thought that the immigrants were taking their jobs and pushing wage levels down. In 1986, when Congress passed the Immigration Reform and Control Act and awarded permanent resident status to undocumented aliens who could prove that they had been living continuously in the United States since 1982, the law brought relief to several million undocumented Mexican workers

Illegal Mexican immigrants being deported by the Border Patrol.

who had been in hiding for years, but it also imposed severe penalties on businesses hiring illegal workers in the future. Early in the 1990s, the Immigration and Naturalization Service proposed building a 6-mile long fence between El Paso, Texas, and Juarez, Mexico, a suggestion that generated vigorous diplomatic protests from Mexico. Many Mexican American activists protested the suggestion as a racist measure.

In addition to Mexican Americans, Puerto Rican Americans, and Cuban Americans, who had long constituted the backbone of the Hispanic community, Central America, South America, and the Caribbean sent millions of people to the United States in the 1980s and 1990s. The immigrants from the Dominican Republic were the most spectacular example, but every other country in Central and South America sent large contingents of immigrants north.

Political instability in Central America explained much of the emigration. Bloody, ideological civil wars between U.S.-backed conservative elites and Communist-backed insurgents made life miserable in El Salvador, Honduras, and Nicaragua during the 1980s, and the fighting did collateral damage to politics and economics in other countries. Only Costa Rica escaped the damage. Journalists dubbed the peasant immigrants "feet people"—comparing them to Vietnamese and Haitian "boat people" who came to the United States via rickety rafts and makeshift vessels—because many walked to the United States. El Salvador sent more immigrants to the United States than any other Central American nation—a total of 220,000 people.

During the 1970s, 1980s, and 1990s, more than 750,000 immigrants from Central America came to the United States. Most of the immigrants from Guatemala settled in southern California, especially Los Angeles, whereas the El Salvadorans and Hondurans preferred Texas and the Gulf Coast. New York City attracted a good number of Hondurans and Panamanians, and large contingents of other Central Americans could be found in Miami, San Francisco, San Diego, and Chicago.

Central America also dispatched several unique ethnic communities to the United States, people who differed considerably from the Spanish-speaking mestizo majority. Large numbers of Mayan Indians immigrated from southern Mexico, Guatemala, and Honduras, and many did not even speak Spanish as their first language. Instead, they spoke Mayan languages, including Kekchi, Cakchiquel, Mopan, and Quiché. And from the Atlantic coast of Central America came Garífuna immigrants. The Garífuna had descended from African slaves who escaped into the mountains of the British colony of Dominica and there married Karib Indians. Their children—Afro-Karibs—became known as Garífunas. Early in the 1800s, British authorities relocated them to British Honduras, today's nation of Belize on the Atlantic coast of central America, and from there they spread south to Honduras and Nicaragua. Some of them immigrated to the United States in the 1980s and 1990s.

Finally, South America dispatched hundreds of thousands of immigrants to the United States in the 1970s, 1980s, and 1990s, including more than 105,000 from Argentina, 70,000 from Chile, 140,000 from Ecuador, 125,000 from Peru, and nearly 40,000 from Venezuela. The largest group of South Americans were Colombians, who in 2000 numbered more than 350,000 people. A small Colombian community had appeared in the Jackson Heights area of New York City after World War II, but during Colombia's political instability in the 1960s and 1970s—known as the era of *la violencia*—the migration accelerated. More than 70,000 Colombians settled in the United States in the 1960s, and another 80,000 in the 1970s. When drug trafficking in the 1980s and 1990s destabilized the government of Colombia and generated even more political violence, the emigration increased, with more than 225,000 Colombians emigrating.

The Colombian immigrants came from diverse backgrounds and settled in the different regions of the United States. As early as 1970, the Colombians in Jackson Heights in Queens called their neighborhood *Chaperino,* and most of the residents were people of European or mestizo (European and Native American) descent, whereas the Colombians who settled in Chicago were *costeños,* or people of

Colombia's Pacific coastal region. They were far more likely than the people of *Chaperino* to be of mixed African, European, and Indian descent. The *costeños* were known for their middle-class values and educated backgrounds.

By the year 2000, the immigration of Spanish-speaking people from the Caribbean, Mexico, Central America, and South America threatened to make Hispanics the largest ethnic minority in the United States. African Americans had long constituted about 12 percent of the American population, or about 30 million people by 2000, but the waves of Hispanic immigrants would soon inundate them. Some demographers predict that by 2006 the number of Hispanics living in the United States will outnumber African Americans.

THE ASIAN MOSAIC

New immigrants also changed the face of the Asian American community. Between 1960 and 2000, more than 1 million Chinese immigrants settled in the United States, bringing the Chinese American community to nearly 2 million people. Unlike earlier Chinese immigrants, who were Cantonese-speaking people from Hong Kong and the southeastern provinces of China, the recent Chinese immigrants tended to be Mandarin-speaking people from the northern provinces of China. The new immigrants often looked down upon the traditions of the older Cantonese settlers, and because so many of them were poor workers employed by Cantonese-speaking business owners, their cultural differences assumed class and political dimensions.

The Japanese American community changed as well, though not because of immigration from Japan. Between 1945 and 1990, approximately 190,000 people immigrated from Japan, but only 37,000 did so in the 1980s and 28,000 in the 1990s. The Japanese American community in the United States totaled 280,000 people in 1941, 465,000 in 1960, 750,000 in 1980, 800,000 in 1990, and 850,000 in 2000. Millions of GIs had returned to the United States in the 1940s, 1950s, and 1960s after being stationed in Japan, and many of them came home with Japanese wives and a great respect for Japanese society. Additionally, in 1988, with passage of the Civil Liberties Act, Congress began paying damages of more than $1 billion to Japanese Americans who had lost their property when they had been interred in relocation camps. For Japanese Americans, the so-called Yellow Power revolved around righting the egregious wrong done to them during World War II. Japanese American activists considered the Civil Liberties Act of 1988 a major civil rights victory, particularly because the law carried a formal apology for the internment camp experience.

Without an infusion of new immigrants from Japan, and with greater acceptance from other Americans, Japanese Americans began to assimilate. By the early 1990s, Japanese American educational levels were second only to those of Jews, and Japanese American family income had become top in the nation. And more than 50 percent of Japanese Americans were marrying non-Japanese.

Until the post-World War II years, Koreans had enjoyed a tiny presence in the United States. Only 9,000 or so Koreans were living here in 1945, but the Korean War from 1950 to 1953 stimulated emigration. Hundreds of thousands of American GIs were stationed in Korea during and after the war, and like many soldiers stationed in Japan, they returned with Asian wives. Those Korean women then arranged for their family members to immigrate, and by 1960 the Korean American community exceeded 50,000 people. In what had a domino effect, the Korean immigrants wrote home praising the virtues and opportunities in the United States, inspiring others to immigrate. More than 270,000 Koreans immigrated in the 1970s, and they were followed by 320,000 people in the 1980s and 340,000 in the 1990s. Los Angeles, with nearly 400,000 immigrants and their children, is the center of Korean American life.

In the United States, Korean immigrants enjoyed extraordinary entrepreneurial success, primarily because of their family-based revolving credit associations known as *kye*, which provided financing for new businesses. Koreans settled in urban areas being abandoned by an earlier generation of immigrants—Jews, Italians, Poles, and the Irish. They opened liquor stores, fast-food restaurants, dry-cleaning establishments, laundries, small grocery stores, pawnshops, floral shops, and video arcades, carving out a niche for themselves in the retail service and convenience industries of run-down urban areas. By 2000, Korean Americans owned more than 20,000 businesses in Los Angeles and thousands more in Chicago and New York City.

But entrepreneurial success came with a price. Korean American businesses in Los Angeles, New York, Chicago, and other cities served a largely African American clientele, and many Blacks resented the success and wondered how such recent immigrants could be doing so well. Korean American businesses survived because of the credit available to them through the *kye* associations and because they employed family members who worked for less than minimum wage and who did not receive any benefits. With very low overhead—below-level wage rates, below-average rents in the depressed commercial real estate markets of the inner cities, and below-market interest rates—Korean American businesses succeeded where others failed.

Tensions between African Americans and Korean Americans exploded in Los Angeles in 1992. When an all-White jury delivered a not-guity verdict in the trial of the Los Angeles police officers accused of beating Rodney King, Black people hit the streets in a rage. Looting and arson became commonplace, and when Los Angeles police could not contain the rioting, Korean American business owners hired Korean American security groups to protect their property. Images of Korean Americans armed with automatic weapons patrolling Korean neighborhoods appeared on television broadcasts throughout the country, highlighting the rancor between the two communities.

But the Filipinos were the most rapidly growing of the Asian immigrant groups. During the 1980s, because the Philippines had one of the world's highest population growth rates and because of the extensive U.S. military presence there, Filipino immigration escalated. U.S. servicemen at Clark Air Base and the Subic Bay Naval Base often married Filipino women, and when they returned home to the United States, their wives arranged for family members to immigrate as well. Approximately 102,000 Filipinos immigrated in the 1960s, with 360,000 arriving in the 1970s, 500,000 in the 1980s, and that same number in the 1990s. By 2000 the Filipino American population had reached approximately 2 million people.

Most Filipinos suffered extreme poverty in the United States, bringing poor educational backgrounds and few job skills when they immigrated. They often worked in unskilled, menial service jobs or as migrant farmworkers. The great Filipino economic success of the 1960s and 1970s came when they organized farmworkers into labor unions. In 1959, the American Federation of Labor had founded the Agricultural Workers Organizing Committee (AWOC) and placed it under the leadership of Larry Itlion, a Filipino American. The AWOC membership was largely Filipino, and in 1966 it joined with César Chávez's National Farm Workers Association to form the United Farm Workers Organizing Committee (UFWOC). After Chávez successfully struck and then boycotted the California growers, Filipino workers benefited when the first labor contracts were signed. Chávez remained head of the union, and Filipino Philip Vera Cruz became vice-president. During the 1980s and 1990s, Filipino migrant workers received modest but very real increases in their wages.

But poverty continued to plague Filipino Americans. Unlike other Asian immigrants, they had no tradition of family rotating credit associations, and without capital, establishing small businesses became extremely difficult. Filipinos also battled internal cultural divisions. Although most Filipinos spoke Tagalog, the Philippines consist of thousands of islands inhabited by people speaking hundreds of languages. Because of internal cultural and linguistic differences, Filipinos had a difficult time marshaling resources to establish self-help institutions. In 2000, Filipino American family income remained among the lowest in the nation.

The Vietnam War and its aftermath during the 1960s and 1970s produced a wave of new Indo-Chinese immigrants—Vietnamese, Cambodians (Khmer), and Laotians (Hmong)—to the United States. The war uprooted millions of people, and eventually more than 1 million of them made their way to America. The infusion of tens of billions of dollars into Southeast Asia transformed the Indo-Chinese economy, prompting millions of people to move to cities where they worked for the U.S. government or for businesses contracting with the United States. This was also true in Thailand, where large U.S. Air Force bases, manned with B-52 bomber crews and technicians, conducted strategic bombing campaigns over Laos, Cambodia, North Vietnam, and South Vietnam. The sheer destruction of the war also forced peasants to move. U.S. forces pursued a policy of attrition in Vietnam, in which military success was measured in enemy body counts. The application of immense firepower in an attempt to destroy enemy troops often proved counterproductive. Because the war was fought largely in Cambodia and South Vietnam, and because it was often difficult to distinguish between ordinary people and enemy troops, civilian casualties mounted into the millions, and Vietnamese, Laotian, and Cambodian peasants fled regions where the fighting was most intense and civilian casualties the highest. Finally, in 1975, when Communist troops overran South Vietnam, Laos, and Cambodia, millions of Vietnamese, Khmers, and Laotians who had worked for the United States, fearing retaliation from the victors, decided to flee their countries. Between 1970 and 1992, approximately 120,000 people came to the United States from Thailand, nearly 140,000 from Cambodia, approximately 190,000 from Laos, and more than 550,000 from Vietnam.

Immigration from Southeast Asia to the United States came in three stages. Until the early 1960s, most Vietnamese, Cambodians, and Laotians in the United States were students enrolled in scientific and engineering programs at American universities. With the U.S. military buildup in South Vietnam, thousands of GIs completing their tours of duty brought Vietnamese wives home with them. Still, by 1975 only 20,038 Indo-Chinese immigrants had settled in the United States. Vietnamese constituted the bulk of the Indo-Chinese immigrants. The numbers of Laotians and Cambodians were so few that the Immigration and Naturalization Service did not bother to keep statistics about them.

The second great migration of Indo-Chinese immigrants commenced in 1975 when North Vietnam completed its conquest of South Vietnam, the Khmer Rouge overran Phnom Penh, Cambodia, and the Pathet Lao seized control of Laos. The refugees who began arriving in the United States were the people who had been closely associated with the anti-Communist regimes of Nguyen Van Thieu in South Vietnam, Lon Nol in Cambodia, and Souvanna Phouma in Laos. The initial wave of 170,000 immigrants arrived in the first year after the Communist takeover and included 155,000 Vietnamese, 7,500 Cambodians, and 7,500 Laotians. Large numbers of them had been employees of the United States or of the overthrown regimes. More than 40 percent of the Vietnamese immigrants were Roman Catholics who had been born in North Vietnam and migrated south in 1954. Most of the Laotians were Hmong tribal peoples who had worked for the Central Intelligence Agency in attacking North Vietnamese troops during the war. By the end of 1975, the United States had taken 130,000 Indo-Chinese refugees at receiving centers in Guam and the Philippines; another 60,000 waited in refugee camps in Hong Kong and the Philippines.

The Vietnamese immigrants tended to be well educated and blessed with good job and professional skills. Many of them also spoke French and/or English. In South Vietnam, they had been large landowners, physicians, dentists, attorneys, civil servants, teachers, small business owners, and employees of large U.S. corporations doing business in South Vietnam. They were accustomed to the economic and social rhythms of modern industrial society, and they had enjoyed substantial contact with Americans during the previous ten years, which limited the culture shock they experienced upon arrival in the United States.

Late in the 1970s, a third wave of Indo-Chinese immigrants began reaching the United States. They were political and economic refugees from the brutal and ineffective policies imposed by the new Communist regimes in Vietnam, Laos, and Cambodia. Vietnamese officials implemented vast collectivization schemes that sent the economy reeling. Ethnic Chinese in Saigon as well as ethnic Khmers in the Mekong Delta were targeted for discrimination, as were the mountain peoples of Laos and Cambodia who had come to Saigon in search of work. The discrimination they faced made all of them likely candidates for emigration. Politically suspect individuals were forced out into reeducation camps in rural areas where they engaged in forced hard labor, received political indoctrination, and participated in mortification programs in which they confessed their sins. In Cambodia, the genocidal maniac Pol Pot instituted a bloody reign of terror that depopulated the country's major cities and towns and led to the deaths of as many as 2 million people.

Third-wave Indo-Chinese immigrants tended to be less educated than the first two contingents, and they were more ethnically diverse, consisting of Vietnamese, Cham, Hmong, Chinese, Khmer, and a variety of mountain peoples. Comparatively few were Roman Catholics.

Many had family members already in the United States. They came out of Vietnam, Cambodia, and Laos illegally, crossing overland through the mountains and jungles of Laos and Cambodia into Thailand, where they ended up in refugee camps.

Most of the Indo-Chinese immigrants who got away after 1976 were boat people who left by sea in small boats, hoping to make it to Indonesia, Thailand, Malaysia, or the Philippines. Approximately 1.3 million people fled Indo-China by boat. On the way, pirates in the South China Sea regularly terrorized them, and Indonesia, Malaysia, and later Hong Kong frequently rejected them even when they did make landfall. Nearly half of those who fled Indo-China by boat died at sea.

At first, Americans welcomed the immigrants with open arms. Congress passed the Indo-Chinese Migration and Refugee Assistance Act of 1975 and renewed the law in 1977, which provided economic assistance to the refugees. The immigrants were systematically settled throughout the United States and not concentrated in one region. Thousands of small and large communities sponsored immigrant families, and the government often contracted the services of local churches and charitable organizations in settling the immigrants into apartments, jobs, and schools. Most Americans, even those who had opposed the war, felt a certain responsibility toward the war's victims. The government paid their airfare to the United States, extended loans to those who wanted to open businesses of their own, and provided scholarships to Indo-Chinese children wanting to attend college. The federal government also provided extra funding to local districts enrolling Indo-Chinese immigrant children.

But their reception was not without challenges. The U.S. economy in the 1970s and early 1980s was weak, characterized by inflation and unemployment, and many American workers resented the competition for jobs the immigrants represented. The country was also full of Vietnam War veterans who did not like the Vietnamese. Also, the mountain people from the Central Highlands of Vietnam and Laos had a difficult time adjusting to the United States. They came from rural backgrounds and found modern urban society alienating. Many went into clinical depressions after their arrival in the United States, and an astonishing number died of a type of sudden-death syndrome. Finally, as time passed, many Vietnamese immigrants moved across the country and began concentrating in certain areas, which also created resentment among Native Americans. By 1992 there were more than 250,000 Hmong and Mien tribespeople from Laos and Montagnards from South Vietnam living in the United States. The Laotians concentrated in Fresno, Sacramento, and Oakland, California. Thousands of South Vietnamese Montagnards settled in North Carolina.

Vietnamese immigrants poured into Orange County, California, and large concentrations of Khmers appeared in the San Diego area.

South Asians—people from India, Pakistan, and Sri Lanka—constituted another new immigrant group in the 1980s and 1990s. Although many Americans, historians and demographers included, described them in the same breath as they did Southeast Asians and East Asians, the South Asians were quite different. Instead of having Buddhist religious backgrounds—like the Chinese, Japanese, and Vietnamese—they were Hindus, Muslims, or Sikhs. During the 1960s, approximately 31,000 South Asians arrived in the United States, but the numbers soon increased dramatically, with 177,000 arriving in the 1970s, 270,000 in the 1980s, and nearly 350,000 in the 1990s.

During the 1860s and 1870s, labor recruiters from Hawaiian sugar plantations brought workers from India, most of them Sikh farmers from the Punjab region. In 1880s, Hawaiian planters replaced the Sikhs with Japanese workers, and Sikh migration fell dramatically. By the early 1900s, many Sikhs in Hawaii and their descendants began moving to the mainland, where they took jobs in railroad construction and commercial farming. The 1920 U.S. census noted 6,400 people of South Asian descent living in the country. Most of them were Sikhs who encountered prejudice and discrimination. They stood out in America for religious reasons, particularly the obligatory "five Ks" of Sikh faith, which every Sikh had to have—*kes* (unshorn hair and beards), *kacch* (knee-length trousers), *kara* (iron bangle), *kirpan* (sword), and *khanga* (hair comb). The Sikh turbans became instantly recognizable to Americans, and although they had roots in Aryan India and were a Caucasian people, their dark skins brought marked discrimination. The American Federation of Labor denounced Sikh immigration in the early 1900s, and anti-Sikh rioting became all too common. The Asian Exclusion League campaigned for a ban on the immigration of Asian Indians. In 1917 Congress agreed and banned them. By 1945, only 1,500 South Asians remained in the United States. At the time of the Immigration and Nationality Act of 1965, approximately 10,000 South Asians lived here.

The South Asian immigrants who came after 1965 differed dramatically from their predecessors. Instead of being Sikhs, most were Hindus and Muslims. Nor were they farm laborers and railroad construction workers. Instead, they were highly educated, urban professionals, an English-speaking middle class often with college degrees. Many of them, especially the Gujaratis, had good business skills and entrepreneurial instincts. In India, they suffered from chronic underemployment and unemployment, even among college graduates. The economy of India simply could not absorb all of the engineers and physicians that universities produced. The South Asians made the most of their opportunities in the United States. By 2000, nearly 60 percent of South Asian immigrants worked as business managers and professionals, including 35,000 physicians and dentists, 55,000 engineers and computer specialists, 25,000 scientists with Ph.D. degrees, 20,000 attorneys, and 18,000 accountants. Tens of thousands of others owned their own businesses—convenience stores, motels, fast-food restaurants, sari shops, and gas stations.

Unlike so many other Asian immigrant groups, the South Asians did not concentrate in specific regions. Perhaps 20 percent lived in the New York City-New Jersey corridor, and locals referred to several blocks on Sixth Street in New York City as "Little India." Another large contingent can be found in Silicon Valley of northern California. But because of their education and jobs skills, Indians have settled all over the country, wherever their careers take them.

Although South Asians have generally found success in the United States, America has sometimes been a mixed blessing because of the discrimination they encounter. The dark skin guarantees some color prejudice, illustrated by the emergence of the epithet "White niggers" to describe them. Also, their Hindu, Muslim, and Sikh faiths contrast sharply with Judaism and Christianity. Many African Americans and Hispanics resent the economic success the South Asians have achieved, and hate crimes against South Asian immigrants increased in the 1990s. The Indian Association of America, a civil rights and ethnic self-help group, has protested the discrimination and works to eliminate stereotyping of Indians and Pakistanis in the United States.

The cultural backgrounds of most Asian immigrants placed a great value on formal personal relations, obedience to authority, and loyalty to family, all of which were threatened by America's emphasis on individual liberty, freedom of expression, and anti-authoritarianism. Many Asian immigrants in the 1980s and 1990s faced an identity crisis in the United States, and although they tried to create a pan-Asian spirit that transcended cultural lines, the basic differences—linguistic, economic, historical, and religious—between Chinese, Japanese, Filipinos, Indo-Chinese, Koreans, and Indians made that impossible to achieve.

Asian Americans became more activist in promoting their civil rights. In the 1970s and 1980s, for example, militant Polynesians in Hawaii founded the Protect Kahoolawe Ohana society to stop U.S. Navy test bombings on the island of Maui, which they considered to be the home of Hina, the sacred rain goddess. Filipino farmworkers continued to be active in farm unions. Groups like the Asian-American Political Alliance and the Intercollegiate Chinese for Social Action campaigned for Asian studies programs on college campuses. The Japanese American Citizens League, the Indian Association of America, the Chinese American Citizens Alliance, and other Asian groups

Betty Ford campaigning at a 1972 Chinese American rally in Chinatown, Los Angeles.

fought negative stereotyping of Asian Americans. They also protested affirmative action policies in California state universities in the 1970s, 1980s, and 1990s that used informal quotas to limit the numbers of Asian students being admitted. The SAT scores of Asian American high school seniors were high enough that they could by themselves fill most of the freshman classes at major California state universities.

MUSLIM AMERICANS

In the 1970s, 1980s, and 1990s, because of immigration from Africa, the Middle East, Central Asia, Indonesia, and South Asia, Islam became one of the fastest-growing religions in the United States. Since the 1870s, the United States had enjoyed an Arab-speaking community of Syrians and Lebanese, but most of them were Christians—either Syrian Orthodox or Roman Catholics of the Uniate tradition. They worked in the textile mill towns of New England and New Jersey, the steel factories of western Pennsylvania and Ohio, the auto factories of Detroit, and the garment district of New York City. Thousands of others worked as peddlers and salesmen and soon made the transition to their own businesses as shopkeepers, wholesalers, and department store owners.

The migration of Muslim peoples to the United States began in the 1880s when small numbers of Arabic-speaking men left the Ottoman Empire—what is today Syria, Jordan, Israel, and Lebanon—and began settling in the factory towns of the Northeast and Midwest. After World War II, the source of Muslim immigrants shifted away from the Middle East and to India, Pakistan, and the Balkans. During the 1960s, Arabic-speaking Muslim immigrants totaled 34,000, whereas only 24,000 came from Afghanistan, Turkey, Pakistan, Iran, and Iraq. But the Immigration and Nationality Act of 1965, which eliminated the old quota system and imposed on each country a maximum of 20,000 immigrants, led to vast increases in the numbers of Muslim immigrants. In the 1970s, 89,000 Arabic-speaking Muslims immigrated, but 130,000 came from non-Arabic regions of the Near East, Central Asia, and South Asia. The change accelerated during the 1980s, when 84,000 Arabic-speaking immigrants were dwarfed in numbers by the more than 260,000 Muslim immigrants arriving from Central Asia, South Asia, and the Soviet Union. In the 1990s, the breakup of the Soviet Union produced several new countries in Central Asia that were overwhelmingly Muslim, and immigrants began arriving from those countries. During that decade, approximately 90,000 Arabic speakers immigrated to the United States, compared to more than 600,000 Muslims from Central Asia, Indonesia, and South Asia.

Finally, political instability in the 1990s in the Balkans sent tens of thousands of Muslim refugees to America. The Serbian-dominated government in the former Yugoslavia began a near-genocidal campaign against its Muslim minority of Bosnians and Kosovars, leaving more than a million people homeless and bringing the military intervention of the United Nations. Milos Korvich, a Bosnian immigrant, remarked to an American journalist in 1999, "I have seen the Statue of Liberty once when we flew from Sarajevo to New York. I will never see it again because I never intend to fly back to that God-forsaken place. I love America."

The Immigration and Nationality Act of 1965 also provided new opportunities for Black Africans. The African immigrants to the United States were a diverse lot, although most came from African nations that had once been colonies of the British Empire, including Sierra Leone, Sudan, The Gambia, Nigeria, Kenya, Somalia, Egypt, and South Africa. A substantial number came from also Eritrea, Ethiopia, and Mali. They were very diverse—Ibo tribesmen from Nigeria who settled on the Gulf Coast; Yorubas from Nigeria who ended up in Midwestern cities, especially Chicago; Wolofs and Mandinkas from West Africa; and Zulus and Xhosas from South Africa. Although many of the Black Africans were Christians or still faithful to their own indigenous traditions, hundreds of thousands were Muslims from northern Ghana, northern Nigeria, southern Mali, southern Chad, and southern Sudan. Islamic mosques sprouted up in large cities and medium-size cities throughout the country.

Muslim immigration increased so dramatically in the 1990s and early 2000s that Muslim Americans soon began to challenge Jewish Americans in numbers. The 2000 census placed the number of American Jews at 6 million, but because of high rates of intermarriage, those numbers were not increasing. Also, Israel had become the destination of choice for Jewish immigrants around the world, and the number of Jews immigrating to the United States had slowed to a trickle. Also, because most Jewish Americans had traditionally been loyal to the Democratic Party, Muslim Americans were more likely to be Republicans, and those loyalties affected United States foreign policy around the world.

Still, the Muslim community in the United States was heterogeneous, divided by history, language, and religious traditions. Although most Arabic-speaking, African, and Balkan Muslims were of the Sunni tradition, Iraqi immigrants were more likely to be Shiites. Large numbers of Muslims from India and Pakistan were of the Ishmaili tradition. Some Muslim immigrants—such as Eritreans, Palestinians, Sudanese, and Pakistanis—remained highly politicized and tied to Old World conflicts, whereas others turned their backs on the Middle East, South Asia, Africa, Indonesia, and Central Asia and prepared to assimilate in their new homeland.

But assimilation for Muslims was not an easy matter. Despite their diversity, many Americans held them in suspicion. Middle East politics reinforced a highly inaccurate image of Muslims as political fanatics. In 1973, during the Yom Kippur War between Israel and several Arab nations, the United States sided with Israel, and in retaliation, the Arab oil-producing nations staged an oil boycott and refused to sell oil to the United States. The Arab oil boycott produced oil shortages and higher energy prices in the United States, and increased American resentment of Arabs in particular and Muslims in general. In 1979 and 1980, when Islamic fundamentalists in Iran seized the U.S. embassy and made hostages of embassy personnel, those resentments increased. Many Americans began to stereotype all Muslims as political fanatics. Other events deepened those biases, such as the taking of American hostages in Lebanon during the 1980s, the terrorist activities of Libyan leader Mu'ammar al-Gadhafi, and the Gulf War of 1991 when the United States and the United Nations went to war against Iraq. In 1999, Islamic fundamentalists bombed the U.S. embassies in Kenya and Tanzania, and in 2000 another group of Islamic radicals bombed the USS *Cole* in Aden,

Yemen. Such overseas controversies frequently expressed themselves politically at home in hate crimes against Muslims and attacks on mosques.

But nothing so challenged Muslim American life as much as the terrorist attacks on September 11, 2001, on the World Trade Center towers in New York City and the Pentagon in Washington, DC. At the instigation of Osama bin Laden and his Al-Qaeda terrorist network, suicide terrorists hijacked four passenger jet aircraft; two of them crashed headlong into the World Trade Center towers, and in the subsequent collapse of the towers, about 3,000 people were killed. Another jet crashed into the Pentagon in Washington, DC, killing more than 180 people. On the fourth hijacked jet, passengers overpowered the hijackers and crashed the aircraft in a field in western Pennsylvania. President George W. Bush then announced a "global war on terrorism."

Most of the terrorists involved in the attacks were radical Muslims who hated American secular culture, the global reach of American power, and American economic, military, and diplomatic support of Israel. But in the wake of the terrorist attacks, many enraged Americans failed to discriminate between the terrorists and the vast majority of Muslims in the United States. Hate crimes against Muslim Americans multiplied in the wake of the September 11th tragedy.

Muslim civil rights organizations worked to counter the stereotypes. The Arab-American Anti-Discrimination Committee protested the stereotyping of Arab Americans in television, film, and other venues of popular culture. The Muslim Association of America, the Organization of Islamic Societies, and the Islamic Society of North America all crusaded for Muslim civil rights and respect for the traditions of religious freedom, and they also worked to disassociate themselves from extremist Islamic factions in the Middle East, the Philippines, Pakistan, and Afghanistan. Given the political instability of those regions, Muslim civil rights activists constantly faced new controversies, and anti-Muslim stereotypes continued to appear frequently in the media.

The Muslim immigrants represented the changing trends in American immigration, the shift away from White European Christians and the rising tide of Asians, Africans, Hispanics, and Middle Easterners. During the 1980s and 1990s, immigration grew dramatically. In the 1990s, an estimated 600,000 immigrants entered the country legally each year, with another 300,000 to 500,000 coming illegally. Between 1980 and 2000, nearly 20 million immigrants had settled in the United States.

Chapter Eight

THE REVOLT OF WHITE ETHNICS

The night started out innocently enough—three White men with a couple of six-packs, a pickup truck, and a tank full of gas, racing up and down the dirt roads and farm-to-market highways of Jasper County, Texas. They spent Saturday night, June 6, 1998, in honky-tonks, swilling beer, telling jokes, and flirting with rheumy-eyed women. With blood-alcohol levels way above the legal limits, they took off for a few more hours of drinking and joyriding. At first glance, Lawrence Brewer, Shawn Berry, and John King appeared to be typical lower-class southern White boys—short on education and long on testosterone—out to have some fun and raise a little hell. So they chug-a-lugged beer, tossed the cans out the window, and careened through Jasper County.

But their joyride soon turned into a racial hate crime of unspeakable dimensions. Shawn Berry, Lawrence Brewer, and John King were not, after all, typical southern boys. All three were convicted felons, and two of them, while in prison, had become active in White supremacist groups and regurgitated racial epithets like the sickies they were. Tattooed swastikas adorned their bodies, and Adolf Hitler lurked in their heads. Life had become a crusade to save East Texas from Blacks, Jews, and immigrants.

In the early morning hours of June 7, they came across James Byrd, a middle-aged Black man who was hitchhiking home from his niece's wedding party. Byrd had had a little too much to drink and in his tipsy condition did not notice the menacing tattoos. He climbed into the truck and waited for the short ride home. They stopped at a convenience store, bought more beer, and then drove back into piney woods. But in the dark, down that country road, they pulled the truck over, hauled Byrd out, and beat him mercilessly. They then hog-tied him. One of the young men suggested tying him to the bumper and dragging him down the road a bit. Drunk on a cocktail of racism and alcohol, they jumped back into the truck and took off; Byrd screamed and pleaded for his life. The boys then accelerated down 2-mile stretch of paved road, with the bumps, culverts, and bridge railings dismembering Byrd piece by piece. Within a time span of three excruciatingly long minutes, Byrd was dead. His dentures, wallet, keys, hat, pieces of clothing, right arm, neck, torso, and head were strewn along the road.

Police solved the crime in a matter of hours. Amid Byrd's severed body parts, they located a cigarette lighter engraved with one of the killer's names. Crime lab specialists found strands of Byrd's hair in the bed of the pickup and his fingerprints on the sidewalls. The truck's tire tracks paralleled the trail of body parts. Eyewitnesses at the honky-tonks and convenience stores put the three killers together that Saturday night and early Sunday morning. When the Jasper County sheriff arrested the three suspects, one of them remarked, confused about all the fuss, "He was just an old nigger."

It was an open-and-shut case. Defense attorneys managed to get change of venues out of Jasper, but in three separate trials, juries found the men guilty of first-degree capital murder. Two were sentenced to death and the third defendant received life without parole. The cold-blooded murder of James Byrd demonstrated clearly for all to see that although the civil rights movement had achieved some success in bringing to pass the American dream of individual liberty and equality, racism and ethnocentrism still thrived in the land of the free and the home of the brave.

THE RISING TIDE OF RACIAL TENSIONS

The Byrd case was symbolic of racial difficulties in the United States at the end of the twentieth century. During the 1990s, although the American economy enjoyed unprecedented prosperity, the flames of racial tensions grew hotter, fueled by the ongoing debates over affirmative action and several high-profile events. Racially motivated hate crimes, like the murder of James Byrd, steadily increased in frequency, and the Ku Klux Klan enjoyed another resurrection. Other White supremacist groups witnessed a growth in membership, and "skinheads"—Black- and Hispanic-hating young White men with shaved heads—became new icons to American racism. David Duke, a former KKK member who campaigned for White rights in Louisiana in the late 1980s and 1990s, enjoyed an astonishing popularity, and right-wing militia movements in the western states often trafficked in racist rhetoric.

Racism, of course, could work both ways. In October 1995, Louis Farrakhan, the controversial leader of the Nation of Islam, or Black Muslims, implemented a "holy day of atonement and reconciliation" for African American men. He invited 1 million Black men to assemble in Washington, DC, and although estimates of just how many participated in the rally varied from several hundred thousand to 1 million, it was certainly the largest gathering of African Americans since Martin Luther King, Jr.'s march in Washington on August 1963. Journalists dubbed the event the "Million Man March." But unlike the Rev. Martin Luther King, Farrakhan's reputation and rhetoric had little in it to inspire White people. Not that he wanted to attract the loyalty of White people. An anti-Semite who regularly blamed Jews for the problems of the world, Farrakhan was also anti-White, although not as blatantly as an earlier generation of Black Muslims. Nevertheless, when White people listened to his speeches, millions came away alienated, somewhat frightened, and less likely to work for racial justice or even to sympathize with its advocates.

The breadth of the racial divide came into clearer focus in the early 1990s. Two Black men—Rodney King and O. J. Simpson—found themselves at the vortex of controversy. In April 1990, Los Angeles police had stopped King on a traffic violation. A relatively benign young Black man with a history of substance abuse and minor scrapes with the law, King was intoxicated and did not cooperate with the officers. Wielding billy clubs like baseball bats, several police officers at the scene attacked King and pounded on him before shackling him in handcuffs and wrestling him into a squad car. Unbeknown to the officers, a bystander armed with a video camera taped the entire event and released the cassette to news outlets. By the next day, the videotape was being played repeatedly by every televison and cable station in the country, and in less than a week 90 percent of Americans over the age of 12 were familiar with the incident.

Early in 1991, the police officers went on trial for assault with a deadly weapon. Defense attorneys managed to get a change of venue out of Los Angeles and up to Simi Valley, a virtually all-White suburb. In April the jury acquitted the police officers. When news of the not-guilty verdict hit the television stations, South Central Los Angeles, home to more than 1 million African Americans, exploded in rage. Tens of thousands of Blacks hit the streets in an orgy of arson and looting. Many White motorists who had accidentally driven into South

Central just after the rioting started were beaten. Although the violence was generally quite random, the stores of Asians, especially Koreans, were targeted for Molotov cocktails. Los Angeles police proved completely incapable of suppressing the rebellion, and the governor of California had to call in national guard troops. After a week, the rioting petered out, but by then fifty-three people were dead and more than $1 billion in property had been destroyed.

In the wake of the rioting, in the neighborhoods bordering South Central, For Sale signs sprouted like crab grass, and White flight to distant suburbs accelerated. The rioting precipitated a vigorous debate throughout the country about race, police brutality, equality, and justice, with liberals arguing that the government needed to promote affirmative action even more aggressively and conservatives calling for law and order. Americans seemed to be singing a racial refrain last heard during the Black Power debates and rioting of the 1960s. Racial feelings became even more strained when the White police officers acquitted of the beating were subsequently indicted, charged, and found guilty in federal court of violating Rodney King's civil rights. Several of the cops drew prison sentences.

The O. J. Simpson case also polarized Americans and acted as an ethnic lightning rod. The former Heisman trophy-winning running back from the University of Southern California and perennial Pro-Bowler and Football Hall of Famer for the Buffalo Bills had become even more of a celebrity after his retirement. Orenthal James "O. J." Simpson made commercials for Hertz rental cars and for Florida orange juice producers, and he acted in a series of hit films. Glib and articulate, with a smile that won the hearts of millions, "the Juice" was a poster child for American opportunity. But he also nursed a near insane jealousy about his former wife, Nicole Brown Simpson, and on several occasions Los Angeles police were called to his home to investigate claims of physical abuse.

When the bodies of Nicole Brown Simpson and her friend Ronald Goldman were found brutally murdered—slashed to death—near her home, O. J. Simpson immediately became the prime suspect. To avoid prosecution, he resisted arrest, and 100 million Americans watched transfixedly as helicopter crews picked up his car driving down a southern California freeway. He eventually turned himself into police and was indicted for double homicide. For most veteran police officers, the evidence of his guilt was overwhelming. His history of spousal abuse supplied the motive, and his Ford Bronco contained blood evidence, confirmed by DNA testing, placing him at the crime scene. On the other hand, the murder weapon was never found.

The trial commenced in the fall of 1994 and dragged on for months into early 1995, with the major television networks, local television stations, and cable outlets broadcasting every word. Americans tuned in by the tens of millions. The vast majority of White Americans concluded that Simpson was guilty, whereas most Blacks were equally convinced of his innocence and that the Los Angeles police department, which had a long history of problems with minorities and corrupt handling of evidence, was out to frame him. Simpson's personal fortune allowed him to hire the so-called dream team of defense attorneys, led by African American Johnnie Cochran, and the defense was able to create reasonable doubt in the minds of jurors. Simpson was acquitted on both counts of murder, and when the verdict was announced, an estimated 100 million Americans and 300 million people around the world were watching. Most White viewers were disgusted, and most Blacks shouted for joy. More than any other event of the 1990s, the O. J. Simpson trial exposed the vast racial gap still afflicting American society.

THE REVIVAL OF WHITE ETHNICITY

With racial tensions on the rise, Americans in the 1980s and 1990s struggled over the meaning of individual rights in a diverse, multicultural society. A changing economy, mass immigration, and fallout over affirmative action all combined to create a racial and ethnic climate of tension and misunderstanding.

The civil rights movement of the 1950s and 1960s, with its rhetoric of racial pride and power, stimulated a revival of ethnic identity and ethnic politics among European immigrants and their descendants. They became more interested in genealogy, family history, and Old World origins. That interest intensified for many Americans in the wake of ABC television's 1977 broadcast of *Roots,* based on Alex Haley's best-selling novel. Travel agents throughout the country marketed tours and vacations promising to put travelers "back in touch with your roots." College and universities added languages to their curriculum because of student interest. In the 1970s, for example, the University of Minnesota expanded its course offerings in Swedish, Norwegian, Danish, and Finnish, with Ohio State University adding courses in Czech, Slovak, and Polish.

White ethnic groups also became more sensitive to ethnic stereotyping and formed watchdog groups to identify discrimination in the media and among politicians. In New York City, Meir Kahane established the Jewish Defense League to combat anti-Semitism and ethnic stereotyping and to promote the cause of Israel in U.S. foreign policy circles. Joseph Colombo founded the Italian-American Civil Rights League to attack negative Italian stereotypes, particularly those that associated Italian Americans with the Mafia. The huge success of the films *The Godfather* and *Godfather II* in the 1970s made that an especially daunting challenge. The Polish American Affairs Council denounced what they called the "slander and ridicule of Polish jokes," insisting that such rhetoric only reinforced false stereotypes and created an atmosphere of political hostility for Poles. B'nai B'rith, which began in the 1870s as a mutual aid society for German Jewish immigrants, evolved over the years into a civil rights group battling anti-Semitism and the negative stereotyping of Jews. Other immigrant groups followed a similar path from mutual aid to civil rights activism, including the National Slovak Society, the National Croatian Society, the Polish National Alliance, the Armenian Educational Association, and the American Hellenic Educational Progressive Association. The revival of White ethnic pride in the 1970s and 1980s could be found on bumper stickers proclaiming "Polish Power" or "Slovak Power" or "Irish Power." "I'm Proud to be Irish" and "I'm proud to be Polish" clubs formed throughout the country.

An ethnic and cultural battle in Denver, Colorado, during the 1990s illustrated the increasing truculence of White ethnics. Since the 1940s, Italian Americans in Denver had staged a parade on October 12 to celebrate Columbus Day, the anniversary of Christopher Columbus's famous voyage across the Atlantic. But Native Americans, who had long resented crediting Columbus with "discovering" the New World, became even more incensed in the 1990s and accused Columbus of committing genocide in the Americas by setting in motion a cycle of disease and conquest that wiped out tens of millions of people. "Letting Italians celebrate Columbus Day," complained a Native American activist, "is no different than if German Americans decided to celebrate Adolf Hitler day with parades, parties, and picnics. It is offensive to Indian people."

For several years in the 1990s the Italian Americans agreed to cancel the parade, but such passive acquiescence left a bitter taste to many Italian immigrants and their descendants. The Italian-American Civil Rights League came to their defense, and in 2000 the parade was rescheduled. On the day of the parade, police officers protecting the parade route almost outnumbered the Italians in the parade and the Indian demonstrators on the sidewalks. "Christopher Columbus was a great man," complained one Italian American to a reporter. "He changed the world forever for the better. Why should we surrender our heritage to a bunch of radical Indians who care more about politics than they do history. The hell with them."

The revival of White ethnicity was, in part, an economic phenomenon. During the 1980s and 1990s, sea changes in the economy had triggered uncertainty and fear. For decades, the number of factory jobs in the United States had steadily declined as the economy made the transition from manufacturing to services. The so-called Rustbelt factories of the Northeast and Midwest became less competitive, less profitable, and less able to sustain high levels of employment. At the same time, the computer revolution was creating millions of new jobs, but jobs in the information industry placed a high premium on technical skills and education, and the acceleration of the new economy left behind the poor, the unskilled, and the uneducated. Many blue-collar workers in the old industries felt bypassed by the booming prosperity, and their resentments often found expression in racism and ethnocentrism.

Many middle-class Americans were caught in the squeeze as well. During the 1980s and 1990s, a rash of corporate mergers and downsizing cost middle managers jobs that had once been secure from the business cycle. Wondering how they had been cut out of the American dream, some middle-class Whites lashed out at minorities, whom they demonized as the source of their own malaise.

Immigrants became a favorite target, especially illegal immigrants who skirted the law by sneaking into the country at the rate of 300,000 people a year. So often in the past, troubled Americans had blamed immigrants for their problems, and the 1980s and 1990s were hardly an exception. Many Whites and Blacks blamed immigrants for public school crowding, burgeoning welfare rolls, exploding demands for public services, and the accompanying tax increases needed to fund them. In response to public concerns, Congress passed the Immigration Control and Reform Act of 1986, which funneled new resources to the Immigration and Naturalization Service and escalated the penalties on employers who hired undocumented workers. In 1990, Congress passed a new immigration act. In what some critics called the "give me your rich and well-to-do elites law," Congress tried to attract the rich and well educated from around the world. Special preferences were handed out to prospective immigrants with money and good educations. As a result, it became easier for Europeans to enter the United States as permanent residents. Some Hispanic, African American, and Asian activists complained abut the legislation.

In 1996 President Bill Clinton signed into law the Illegal Immigrant Reform and Immigration Responsibility Act, which proved almost draconian in its impact on illegal immigrants. The law provided for the deportation of noncitizens with criminal records, regardless of how serious the offense or how long ago it had occurred. It increased funding to the Immigration and Naturalization Service (INS), and within a year the INS became the federal government's largest law enforcement agency. The legislation provided criminal penalties for any illegal immigrant who reentered the United States within a ten-year period of his or her deportation. Finally, illegal immigrants arriving without proper documentation could be deported immediately without having to appear before an immigration judge.

The impact of the Illegal Immigrant and Immigration Responsibility Act of 1996 was immediate and widespread. Tens of thousands of illegal immigrants who had lived for long periods in the United States were deported. Many of them had married U.S. citizens and had children who were U.S. citizens. The deportations broke up families and threw thousands of them on the welfare roles. Congressman Barney Frank of Massachusetts pilloried the law: "They couldn't crack down on legal immigration . . . so they decided to make it as tough as possible for those already here."

Other laws also targeted poor, uneducated immigrants. In 1994 California voters approved Proposition 187, which required state officials to deny public services—welfare benefits, access to public hospitals, and desks in public schools—to illegal immigrant workers and their families. Hispanic leaders quickly filed lawsuits against the legislation, labeling it a violation of civil rights and equal protection under the law. The lawsuit suspended enforcement of the legislation until the federal courts could rule on its constitutionality. In 1998, California voters approved Proposition 227, which forced local school districts to abandon bilingual education programs in favor of a "total immersion English curriculum." Other states, especially in the Southwest, followed suit.

In 2001, however, two U.S. Supreme Court decisions stemmed some of the anti-immigrant tide. In *Immigration and Naturalization Service v. St. Cyr,* the federal government argued the right to expel, without due process or court review, immigrants who had committed crimes. And in *Zadvydas v. Davis,* the government argued that it could indefinitely incarcerate immigrants scheduled for deportation if their countries of origin would not take them back. But in its decisions, the Supreme Court found that immigrants living in the United States are "persons" under the U.S. Constitution and therefore are protected by the Bill of Rights. Denying immigrants court reviews and incarcerating them for indefinite terms, the court decided, violated their Fifth and Fourteenth Amendment rights to due process.

AFFIRMATIVE ACTION IN RETREAT

The combined impact of affirmative action, mass immigration, and rising racial tensions produced a White political backlash in the United States. During the 1950s and early 1960s, the civil rights coalition functioned largely within the Democratic Party and revolved around African Americans, Roman Catholics, Jews, and blue-collar workers; they had unitedly battled against the *de jure* segregation that so blatantly contradicted the values of the Declaration of Independence and the Bill of Rights. But Supreme Court decisions and laws like the Civil Rights Act of 1964 and the Voting Rights Act of 1965 could not eliminate racism or address the question of poverty. Equality and economic security proved to be difficult to achieve.

Civil rights activists and Black Power proponents began to focus on *de facto* discrimination, and the riots of the 1960s exhibited the depth of resentment and rage residing in the hearts of many African Americans. To accelerate an end to *de facto* discrimination and poverty, the federal government in the late 1960s, 1970s, and 1980s adopted several controversial policies that served to alienate large numbers of Whites in the civil rights coalition. The most divisive policies included redesigning electoral districts to promote racial balances among elected officials, busing children across school district lines to achieve racially integrated schools, enforcing open housing laws, subordinating seniority rights to those of recently hired minority workers, and imposing racial quotas on the admissions, hiring, and promotion policies of universities, local governments, and private businesses.

But the attempt to reverse the effects of three centuries of racial discrimination collided head on with several centuries of immigration, community building, and civil rights consciousness among Whites. As part of a peasant heritage brought with them from Europe, the immigrants became profoundly committed in the United States to their homes, families, and neighborhoods, which included their houses, parishes, synagogues, schools, parks, and playgrounds. Many Whites viewed affirmative action programs, open housing laws, and school busing as assaults on their neighborhoods. In the troubled economy of the 1970s and early 1980s, they grew incensed at limits on union seniority rules. And in the affirmative action regulations shaping college admissions rules, they saw limits on the ability of their own children to secure access to higher education.

Several concrete assumptions formed the heart of White ethnicity. Pluralism and multiculturalism, White ethnics argued, were not just racial phenomena but could be ethnic as well and could also revolve around issues of national origins and religion. To be sure, the forces of assimilation were working on White ethnic groups, but decades and even centuries would pass before any single melting pot absorbed Whites into a single community. They demanded respect from others and insisted that the achievement of civil rights and equality for some people should not involve the socially engineered destruction of the neighborhoods and institutions of others. White ethnic leaders generally believed that racial and ethnic groups had to maintain themselves voluntarily and that government should approach them the same way it had historically approached religious groups—doing nothing either to promote, to limit, or to destroy them. It was not the purpose of government, they insisted, to sponsor residential, educational, or occupational dispersion programs, especially when and where little evidence existed of overt discrimination in the past.

Most White ethnics refused to accept blame for the economic plight of minorities and were quick to reply that they had not even been in the United States during the age of slavery and were responsible for neither segregation nor urban ghettoes. In fact, most of the Polish, Italian, Slovak, Greek, Lithuanian, Russian, Jewish, Serbian, Croatian, Slovenian, Romanian, and Hungarian immigrants had arrived in American cities just when Blacks and Hispanics were settling there, and they too had encountered a fair measure of discrimination. Many Whites simply refused to accept personal blame for slavery, Jim Crow segregation, and racism. And instead of viewing affirmative action, busing, racial gerrymandering of district lines, and restrictions on union seniority rules as legitimate means of achieving equality, they saw them as reverse discrimination and illegitimate attempts to destroy neighborhoods and communities. When Polish Roman Catholics in Detroit or Irish Catholics in South Boston protested school busing, or when Hasidic Jews in Brooklyn objected to federal electoral redistricting, or when labor unions sued to protect seniority rights, they did not consider their opposition to be *prima facie* evidence of racism.

Resentment of what they felt was reverse discrimination deepened in the 1980s and 1990s. White ethnic leaders interpreted the Constitution—especially the First, Fifth, and Fourteenth Amendments—in individual, not group, terms. The Constitution, they insisted, was designed to protect an individual, not a group, from discrimination and to guarantee an individual, not an entire ethnic group, equal protection under the law. The efforts of the federal government to guarantee equality were perfectly legitimate if they removed *de jure* obstacles and created a level playing field where equal opportunity for every American prevailed. But if government entered into formal partnerships with certain ethnic groups at the expense of others, it became a co-conspirator in racial and ethnic discrimination and undermined the real meaning of the Constitution.

The federal courts soon began to agree. The Supreme Court's 1978 decision in *University of California Board of Regents v. Bakke* marked the beginning of the decline of affirmative action in the United States. Alan Bakke, a White male, had applied for admission to the medical school at the University of California at Davis. He was denied admission in 1973 and in 1974, even though his grade point average and score on the medical school admissions tests were higher than those of several minority applicants who had been admitted. To comply with affirmative action dictates from the federal government, the medical school admissions committee had established fixed racial quotas, guaranteeing admission to sixteen minority candidates regardless of their grade point averages or medical school admission test scores. Bakke asserted that such quotas discriminated against him as a White male. Had he been Black or Hispanic or Native American, Bakke asserted, he would have been admitted. Conversely, the only reason he had been denied admission was because of his race and gender. In establishing such admission standards, the University of California, he claimed, had violated his Fourteenth Amendment right to equal protection under the law.

Not surprisingly, when Bakke filed his lawsuit against the University of California, the White ethnic community rallied to his side. Legal briefs supporting his constitutional position were filed in federal court by the American Jewish Committee, the American Jewish Congress, the Italian-American Foundation, the Italian-American Civil Rights League, the Polish-American Affairs Council, the Polish-American Educators Association, the Hellenic Bar Association, the Ukrainian Congress Committee of America, and the Slovak Society. Each of these groups agreed that *de jure* discrimination against individuals on the basis of race, religion, or national origin was unconstitutional, but they also insisted that rigid government quotas based on those same criteria discriminated against individuals not included in the arbitrary arrangement. They pledged allegiance to the ideas of pluralism and equality of opportunity but refused to define that in terms of groups. Nor were they willing to endorse government programs that damaged communities and neighborhood schools in the name of freedom.

The case of *University of California Board of Regents v. Bakke* reached the U.S. Supreme Court and was decided on June 28, 1974, by a five to four vote, which certainly reflected how divided the country was over affirmative action. The decision came down in Bakke's favor, agreeing that he had indeed been robbed of his civil rights, particularly under Title VI of the Civil Rights Act of 1964. By establishing rigid racial quotas in its admission policies, the University of California had unwittingly engaged in reverse racial discrimination—that had Bakke been a minority and not a White man, he most certainly would have been admitted. Such reverse discrimination, the majority opinion concluded, was unconstitutional. Affirmative action programs, the court continued, could not employ fixed racial quotas in establishing admission, hiring, and promotion standards.

Critics of affirmative action hailed the *Bakke* decision as a victory for civil rights and the Constitution. Senator John Tower of Texas remarked, "I am delighted that the justices have finally seen the light. Discriminating against one group of people to end discrimination against another group does nothing in the long run to end discrimination." Backers of affirmative action did take some comfort in the decision, because the court had ruled that government agencies could still take race into account in their admissions, hiring, and promotion policies. Benjamin Hooks, head of the National Association for the Advancement of Colored People, called *Bakke* a "clear-cut victory for voluntary affirmative action." But a disappointed Thurgood Marshall, who had voted with the court's minority in the decision, recognized the full import of *Bakke:* "The tide has turned," he said, "and I suspect it won't be coming back for a long time. I fear the cause has sustained a mortal wound." Other civil rights advocates, such as Georgia state legislator Julian Bond and the Rev. Jesse Jackson, head of PUSH (People United to Save Humanity), condemned the *Bakke* decision as a setback for the civil rights movement.

With the *Bakke* decision, affirmative action plateaued as a political movement. *Bakke* was the first in a series of judicial and political decisions that became a trend to ensure that affirmative action did not discriminate against White men. The depth of the discontent with affirmative action among White ethnics became abundantly clear in the 1980s when many of them became so-called Reagan Democrats. In the presidential elections of 1980, 1984, and 1988, Republican presidential candidates made substantial gains in the blue-collar neighborhoods of Chicago, Cleveland, Buffalo, St. Louis, Minneapolis, Pittsburgh, Philadelphia, Baltimore, and Cincinnati. Republican candidates were more outspoken in their opposition to affirmative action quotas than Democrats, and their criticism resonated among many blue-collar workers who could usually be counted on to vote Democrat. The Republican Party's success in taking control of both houses of Congress in 1994 could largely be attributed to their new-found success among southern Whites and northern White ethnics. Under Presidents Reagan and Bush, the Equal Employment Opportunity Commission, which investigated complaints of civil rights violations, experienced relative budget declines, and lack of funds prevented vigorous enforcement of affirmative action regulations.

Just how many Americans resented affirmative action became abundantly clear to President Bill Clinton in the spring of 1993 when he nominated Professor Lani Guinier of the University of Pennsylvania to lead the civil rights division of the Department of Justice. A brilliant, African American legal scholar, Guinier was on the philosophical cutting edge of affirmative action theory, and in some of her writings she had speculated that election outcomes, not just election procedures and regulations, might constitute evidence of racial discrimination. Even if the conduct of elections appeared to be aboveboard and fully compliant with the law, the inability of minority candidates to be elected in numbers proportionate with their population might still be the result of racial discrimination.

Her nomination precipitated a political firestorm. Critics of affirmative action unfairly accused Guinier of promoting election outcome quotas, in which certain numbers of minority candidates had to be guaranteed election victory even if they did not have the votes. "If she ends up at justice," argued one conservative radio talk show host, "we will have 'minority set-aside' elections in which quotas of political offices are reserved for women and minorities. Maybe we ought to just cancel elections and let the NAACP and the National Organization for Women appoint congressmen and senators." The political controversy grew so heated that Guinier's nomination never even made it to the Senate Judiciary Committee for confirmation. President Clinton had to withdraw the nomination.

Large-scale immigration in the 1980s and 1990s further undermined affirmative action. With so many millions of immigrants flowing into the country from Latin America, Asia, and Africa, the size of minority groups—and the number of people eligible for affirmative action—swelled. The American-born daughter of a Nigerian immigrant, for example, was a U.S. citizen *and* an African American before the law. As a minority and as a woman, she qualified for affirmative action benefits, and many Whites resented it. One California legislator in 1998 remarked, "I used to support affirmative action because I know that racism has been a fact of American life and millions have suffered. We do need to make up for past discrimination. But why should the children of recent immigrants, even if they are U.S. citizens, be eligible for affirmative action. Must we also atone for the sins of the entire world?"

The backlash forced local and state governments to dismantle a number of affirmative action programs. In cities and states around the country during the 1990s, opponents of affirmative action worked in the courts and through local ballot initiatives to overturn affirmative action. In 1998, California voters approved Proposition 209, which scrapped affirmative action programs in state government and higher education by prohibiting universities from considering race as a factor in admission, hiring, promotion, or the awarding of contracts. Although proponents of affirmative action challenged Proposition 209 in the federal courts, the measure survived, and instead of race, the state government began to use economic disadvantage as a criterion in making admissions, hiring, and promotion decisions.

Judicial trends also continued in the direction marked by *Bakke.* White men filed lawsuits against affirmative action regulations, and many of them succeeded. In 1989, for example, the U.S. Supreme Court heard the case of *Ward's Cove Packing Co. v. Antonio,* which dealt with job discrimination. Until the *Ward* case, if statistical analysis demonstrated that disproportionate numbers of minorities and women were excluded from certain jobs, the company had to prove that the job qualifications were work related and a "business necessity." In their decision, the court by a narrow five to four majority shifted the burden of proof in such discrimination cases from the employer to the employees.

Another 1989 Supreme Court decision damaged the affirmative action minority set-aside programs, which guaranteed that minority contractors received a certain percentage of government contracts, regardless of whether they were low bidders. The city of Richmond, Virginia, by city council ordinance reserved 30 percent of all public works appropriations for minority-owned construction companies. In the case of *Croson v. City of Richmond,* the U.S. Supreme Court ruled that such a city ordinance was unconstitutional because it violated the Fourteenth Amendment right to equal protection under the law of White contractors.

In 1995, the Supreme Court took a look at a broad spectrum of affirmative action regulations, hearing the case of *Adarand v. Pena,* which dealt with affirmative action programs in general and whether they would continue indefinitely in the United States. In its decision, the court ruled consideration of race or ethnicity in federal affirmative action initiatives was legal, but that judges had the right to subject those initiatives "to the highest level of judicial scrutiny" and must be narrowly crafted to serve what the court called an "overwhelming and compelling interest." Most legal observers concluded that *Adarand* constituted a setback for affirmative action.

Even more damaging to the future of affirmative action was *Hopwood v. Texas,* decided in 1997 by the fifth circuit court of appeals. Cheryl Hopwood and three other Whites who had been denied admission to the University of Texas Law School claimed that their Fourteenth Amendment rights to equal protection under the law had been violated by UT's affirmative action admission rules. Their test scores and grade point averages had been higher than ninety-three African Americans and Mexican Americans who had been admitted. The court prohibited the University of Texas from employing race as a factor in awarding financial aid, admitting students, and hiring and promoting faculty members. Higher courts refused to review the decision, and colleges and universities throughout the country were forced to alter their policies in the light of *Hopwood.* Donald Stewart, president of the College Board, warned that in *Hopwood* "we're looking at a potential wipeout that could take away an entire generation." And in the wake of *Hopwood,* minority enrollment in professional schools declined.

Still, although formal affirmative action regulations were under assault, affirmative action values by the 1990s had become part of the culture of colleges, universities, government agencies, and major corporations throughout the country. Most Americans did see the value of diversity and the need for educational institutions, companies, and government agencies at all levels to reflect that diversity. In Texas, for example, state and federal officials in May 2000 worked out an agreement to establish top-quality, high-demand academic programs by improving facilities at such traditionally Black institutions as Prairie View A&M University and Texas Southern University and at such historically Hispanic institutions as the University of Texas-Pan American. Similar agreements guaranteed an upgrading of facilities at Cheyney University of Pennsylvania and Kentucky State University, two traditionally Black institutions. Fortune 500 corporations throughout the country actively recruited minority candidates, as did federal and state agencies.

It was, however, a complex endeavor. In 1992, for example, the U.S. Supreme Court rendered its decision in the *United States v. Kirk Fordice* case, ordering the state of Mississippi to discontinue its policies that kept higher education institutions racially identifiable. The decision meant that more African American students needed to enroll at historically White institutions such as the University of Mississippi and more White students needed to enroll at historically Black schools such as Alcorn State University. Bringing such enrollment changes to pass proved difficult. In 1995, for example, a federal district court ordered the state of Alabama to establish White-only scholarships as a means of attracting White students to Alabama A&M University and Alabama State University, two historically African American institutions. The availability of full tuition rides, the federal judge assumed, would convince White students to apply and enroll. But a graduate student sued, arguing that reserving a certain quota of scholarships for Whites constitutes racial discrimination against Black, Hispanic, and Native American students. At the end of the twentieth century, Americans had still not managed to solve their nagging racial and ethnic problems.

Despite the series of unfavorable court decisions, civil rights advocates insisted that affirmative action had succeeded in blunting some of the effects of racism. In the mid-1990s, an expert in the Department of Labor concluded that "more than 16 million women and people of color occupied higher occupational categories than if affirmative action had never existed." The National Employers Lawyers Association claimed that "as long as there is discrimination based on race, national origin, and gender, we must use remedies and undertake voluntary actions that take race, ethnicity and gender into account. We must acknowledge that such efforts have been proved essential and must remain if we are to achieve this nation's promise of equal opportunity."

Chapter Nine

ETHNIC AMERICA AT THE TURN OF THE MILLENNIUM

Fishermen pulled the 6-year-old boy from the shark-infested waters of the Florida Straits on Thanksgiving Day, 1999. Clinging to an inner tube, he was the only survivor of a group of desperate Cubans who had set sail in a rickety, home made boat that had foundered in deep water. Elián Gonzales's mother had fled Cuba with her boyfriend, hoping to build a new life in the United States. No sooner had the fishermen brought Elián to Miami than the press jumped on the story. The boy was emaciated and badly sunburned, and his cow-eyes revealed little more than the shock he had sustained in seeing so many people die, including his mother. The Immigration and Naturalization Service placed Elián in Miami with relatives, who agreed to care for him until permanent arrangements could be made. He thrived in their home. With his creamy brown skin, big brown eyes, and impish grin, Elián Gonzales captured the heart of the nation and instantly became the foster child of the United States.

He also became swept up in the tornado of Cold War and American presidential politics. Elián's Miami relatives loathed Fidel Castro and claimed that the boy needed to be given political asylum in the United States. After all, his mother had died trying to bring him to freedom. Many Americans, however, wondered how a 6-year-old boy could claim political asylum or be subjected to political persecution were he returned to the island. He spent his mornings in Miami watching *Teletubbies* and cartoons on television. His relatives took him to Disneyworld and bought him more toys than a hundred Cuban children would ever see. He appeared to be happy and content, at least as far as news reports went. Back in Cuba, however, Elián's father wanted the boy returned to his custody. And by any measure, the father was a hardworking, kind man who loved his country and his son and wanted to live out his life in Cuba. Any domestic court judge in the United States would have turned the boy immediately over to his biological father. Custody should have been an open-and-shut case.

But 2000 was a presidential election year, and both the Republicans and the Democrats wanted to lay claim to Florida's electoral votes. The Cuban American community in Miami, rabidly anti-Castro, campaigned in the courts and in the media to keep Elián in Miami, and Republican presidential candidate George W. Bush generally agreed with them. The Texas governor knew how to count votes, and he could not afford to offend Cuban Americans, who generally voted Republican. The Bill Clinton administration, however, was inclined to follow immigration law, which determined that Elián was not old enough to make a case for his own asylum and that he should be handed over to his father.

During the first half of 2000, the case moved its way through the federal courts, but in July, when the federal courts finally ordered the Miami relatives to hand the boy over, they refused, barricading themselves in their home. Attorney General Janet Reno ordered federal marshals to seize him, and in an early morning raid covered by the world media, the terrified little boy was taken at gunpoint. Photographs of the marshals storming the house were printed around the world. Elián's father came to the United States to pick up his son, and the reunion was a joyful one, convincing most Americans that sending the boy back to his family in Cuba was the wise choice. In Cuba, Fidel Castro enjoyed a propaganda field day over the controversy, accusing the "imperialistic" United States of "kidnapping," and in Cuba his charges resonated well with the masses. Like most Americans, Cubans knew instinctively that Elián should be raised at home by his father. Whatever hope the United States in general, and Cuban Americans in particular, nurtured for Castro's political demise was shattered. He had stood up to the United States and won, bringing Cuba's little boy back home, and the country hailed him. In summer 2000, the incident had given Cuba two genuine heroes: Fidel Castro and Elián Gonzales.

In mixing Old World politics with New World concerns, the Elián Gonzales case was hardly pioneering new ground. Many Jewish and Arab Americans track Mideast politics today like bookies following a betting line, and in the late 1980s, when the satellite nations of eastern Europe left Moscow's orbit, Americans of Lithuanian, Estonian, and Latvian descent celebrated the Soviet demise. So did Polish Americans, Romanian Americans, Hungarian Americans, Czech Americans, and Slovak Americans when the Soviet Union disintegrated in 1991. As Yugoslavia broke up in the 1990s, many Americans of Serbian, Bosnian, Croatian, Slovenian, and Kosovar descent followed the events closely and tried to exert political pressure on the Clinton administration. French Canadians in New England sympathized with the Quebec radicals who wanted to secede from Canada, and in 2000, many Mexican immigrants living in the United States were allowed to vote in Mexico's presidential election. Native Americans sympathized with the Mayan Indians rebelling in Chiapas, Mexico, while Pakistani and Indian immigrants worried about the border wars on the subcontinent. For immigrants and ethnic minorities to be concerned about Old World events and their New World ramifications is as old as American history.

An Immigrant Culture

Except for India, the United States in the year 2000 appears to be the most ethnic country in the world—a nation for whom diversity has all but become an icon, a condition not to be feared but to be revered and worshiped. Within the larger context of individual liberty and equal economic opportunity, cultural pluralists exalted ethnic differences as the genius of American society. Congressman Tip O'Neill of Massachusetts, whose ancestors came from Ireland, once said, "My heart is shaped like a shamrock and I bleed Irish green, but my world and my family have become a rainbow of people from all over the world. God how I love America!"

For much of the twentieth century, historians had looked to the frontier experience to explain the past and illuminate the American character, particularly the value Americans invested in hard work, self-reliance, and personal independence. But immigration could just as easily explain those values, and immigration was far more enduring than the frontier and the vast open spaces of the West. When the U.S. census announced in 1890 that the frontier no longer existed, the immigrants kept coming, by the millions and tens of millions, and although they may have been different in terms of language, skin color, and religion than earlier generations of immigrants, they were also the same.

In many ways, a Scottish-Irish immigrant leaving northern Ireland in 1740 was exactly like a Gujarati immigrant departing India in 1999. A Haitian immigrant trying to cross the Caribbean in 2000 had much in common with a Mexican immigrant traversing to cross the Rio Grande in 1945 or a Chinese immigrant voyaging across the Pacific Ocean in 1849. Most immigrants tend to share certain personality traits and certain attitudes, regardless of race, religion, color, or national origin, and regardless of the century when they arrived in the United States. Each new contingent of immigrants—in the 1630s or 1840s or 1920s or 1990s—serves to replenish those values and characteristics in American society and provides an ongoing cultural continuity. In 1782, J. Hector St. Jean de Crevecoeur wrote, "The American is a new man who acts on new principles; he must therefore entertain new ideas and form new opinions." And it is immigration that has allowed and continues to allow Americans to reinvent themselves, to become new men and women and to entertain new ideas and form new opinions.

Today, prospective immigrants queue up outside U.S. embassies throughout the world. The men and women waiting in line are anxious to secure residence visas so they can immigrate to the United States, and most of them are young and healthy. Relatively few are senior citizens. Historically, the elderly and the infirm did not immigrate, and today is no different. It takes too much energy and requires migrants to leave comfort zones, abandon old habits, and defy tradition. Older people, more set in their ways and resistant to change, hold back and stay home, figuring that what they know in the Old World is preferable to what they do not know about the new. A 70-year-old Irish Catholic caught in the potato famine of 1844–1845 was no more likely to leave Ireland than an 80-year-old Filipino suffering in poverty on the island of Mindanao. Immigration, yesterday and today, is the business of the young.

Immigrants also tend to be hard workers; lazy people usually do not, nor did they ever, leave the country of their birth for a new life abroad. They prefer to stay home and endure their miseries rather than invest time, energy, and money in traveling across the world and settling in America. Once in the New World, immigrant survival required backbreaking work on farms or in factories, and more often than not, when immigrants spoke no English, they found themselves underemployed, working long hours just to survive. Whether an Irish Catholic laying track for the Union Pacific Railroad in the 1860s or a contemporary Cambodian running a donut shop in Los Angeles, immigrants have usually found themselves working long days, six days a week, making ends meet through the sweat of their brow. Leisure time has never been a commodity new immigrants could afford.

More than the people they left behind in the Old World, immigrants often nursed streaks of rebellion, an unwillingness to always do what they had been told or to always do what was expected. They tend to be an impatient people unwilling to wait for blessings in heaven. In eighteenth- and nineteenth-century Europe, for example, children often inherited the occupations of their fathers and had little discretion to do otherwise. For the sons of carpenters who did not want to be carpenters or the sons of masons who did not want to spend their lives working with brick and mortar, emigration became one way of breaking tradition and building a new, different life, even if it meant defying convention. Many prospective immigrants also faced strong family pressures not to leave for the New World. In the 1700s and 1800s, emigration usually constituted a permanent good-bye to family and friends; immigrants rarely returned home for visits. "When I waved good-bye to my mother at the docks in Arundal," remembered Lars Sorensen, a Norwegian immigrant who settled in Superior, Wisconsin, in 1887, "I knew I would never see her again. My heart sank, but I would not, I could not, spend the rest of my life working the God-forsaken, rock-strewn soil in Norway. I would have died of discouragement."

Immigrants also tend to be optimistic risk-takers. Conservative, cautious people preoccupied with what might go wrong in their life never take the chance to immigrate. When Lars Sorensen informed his father of his decision "to go to Wisconsin, North America," his father replied, "My God, boy, you're crazy. It's a land of savages. They'll kill you and drink your blood. Mark my words. You will rue the day you ever decided to leave Norway." Confidence is and always has been an epidemic disease among immigrants, who are convinced that chances are worth taking and risks worth being endured. Immigration explains much about the legendary American faith in the future, the belief that progress is inevitable and failure quite impossible.

Finally, most immigrants have been pragmatic people, willing to stretch or break the rules in order to get to the United States and stay here. Over the centuries, they have fled legally binding apprenticeships, indentured servitude, debts, and the military draft to get here; to stay here they have often exercised creative manipulation of the law, whether getting by on forged documents, staging sham marriages, or staying one step ahead of Immigration and Naturalization Service agents. Late in the nineteenth century, philosopher William James argued that pragmatism was a quintessential American virtue— an attitude that defined the culture; most immigrants have not only fit in to the culture but have served to reinforce it.

Today, the immigrant personality remains quite consistent with history. Whether it's a Mexican immigrant crossing the Rio Grande into Texas, a Salvadoran avoiding border patrol agents in Los Angeles, a Haitian plying the dangers of the Caribbean in a rickety raft to make landfall in South Florida, or a Chinese student trying to secure a work visa, they tend to be the same as the tens of millions of immigrants who have preceded them to the United States. They are young and hardworking, willing to bid friends and family good-bye, sometimes forever, in order to make their way to America. They tend to be unusually optimistic, hopeful people, confident that their plans will work out, that the risks will be worth the rewards, that America will deliver on its promise. And what today's immigrants do, as have their predecessors, is continuously infuse the national psyche, filling up the American reservoir with ambition, confidence, and pragmatic flexibility. In some ways, before they ever leave home, they have already become Americans.

THE MELTING POT

For all the political controversy surrounding immigration and affirmative action and high-profile ethnic events like the O. J. Simpson trial, the Rodney King beating, and the Elián Gonzales case, however, the great American melting pot continues to work its magic—gradually, slowly, and imperceptibly absorbing most ethnic communities and producing new types of ethnic identity. The forces of assimilation do their work surreptitiously, almost invisibly, even though, at any given time, American society seems to drip ethnicity. Today, the streets of Jackson Heights in Queens, New York City, resemble the Dominican Republic, with the sounds, smells, and sights of the island. Miami's Little Havana, except for its economic prosperity, might as well be a section of the real Havana. Parts of West Los Angeles resemble Teheran, Iran. Along West 46th Street in Manhattan or out in Astoria in Queens, Brazilian immigrant culture is readily visible. And East Los Angeles, except for Mexico City, is the largest Mexican city in the world. In any number of cities in the United States, or on Native American reservations, ethnic diversity is common.

To be sure, large pockets of foreign language communities still thrive. For Mexican Americans, Cuban Americans, Dominican Americans, and Puerto Rican Americans, Spanish is the primary language for many and a secondary language for most. Italian can still be heard on the streets of New York City, as can Polish in Chicago, German in Milwaukee, French in the Cajun country of southwestern Louisiana and upper New England, Korean and Farsi (Iranian) in Los Angeles, and Chinese—Cantonese and Mandarin—in San Francisco, New York, and Honolulu.

But visible diversity does not mean that assimilation has stalled. For every immigrant bringing new cultural institutions into the United States, descendants of previous immigrants are disappearing into the mainstream. Historically, when immigrants arrived in the United States, they encountered values that contrasted sharply with those of the Old World: the emphasis on the individual rather than the community, the premium on success and progress rather than on survival, the elevation of the material rather than the spiritual, the supremacy of secular rather than religious values, the replacement of stability with every kind of mobility, the loss of the Old World language in favor of English, the liberation of women and children from patriarchal authority, and the transformation of diverse folk religions into larger denominational traditions. As they lost the Old World language, religious folkways, family values, and political loyalties in favor of American culture, their sense of community expanded.

During the early years of the twentieth century, for example, as immigration from Germany, Scandinavia, and the British Isles tapered off, national origin identities lost much of their pull. Second- and third-generation Norwegian Americans, for example, tended to lose interest in Old World politics and were far less inclined than their parents and grandparents to join such organizations as the Sons of Norway. Without large numbers of immigrants arriving annually, membership in immigrant societies steadily declined. And as English became the first language of the children and grandchildren of Norwegian immigrants, another link to the Old World was severed. Subscriptions to Norwegian language newspapers declined precipitously, and many publications went out of business. What happened to the British, Germans, and Scandinavians in the early 1900s happened after World War II to the descendants of immigrants from eastern and southern Europe. Ethnic identities based on national origins in the Old World and Old World languages steadily eroded.

Each immigrant group tried to preserve its ethnic heritage, but it was a losing cause. The democratic individualism, secular values, ethnic diversity, geographic and occupational mobility, and mass culture of America made acculturation a relentless process. Language was usually the first victim. English was the language of public society—government, public school, mass media, and the economic marketplace. To function in public society, the immigrants and their children had to learn English. Churches, parochial schools, and immigrant societies tried to counter the public language in private settings, but by the time the second generation had established its own families, English had usually become the language of intimacy at home. For third-generation children, English was the mother tongue, and whatever familiarity they had with the Old World language was often a consequence of formal instruction at school rather than native ability. Even then, whatever connection they had with their grandparents' language was more an academic than a functional, cultural bilingualism.

As the ties to the Old World weakened, the centrifugal forces of American society fueled the forces of assimilation. During World War II, tens of millions of Americans had been forced to leave the neighborhoods settled by their families and ethnic compatriots and relocate to distant places. Young men by the millions joined the military during the war and left the ethnic communities of the Northeast and Midwest for military bases in the South and West. The war launched a demographic shift of momentous proportions that gave rise to the Sunbelt. Between 1950 and 2000, the northern states enjoyed only modest population gains, while the states of the South and West witnessed geometric increases in population. In the cities of the South and West—Atlanta, New Orleans, Houston, Dallas, San Antonio, Phoenix, San Diego, Seattle, Denver, and Los Angeles—the children and grandchildren of European immigrants found themselves living in mixed neighborhoods where Old World identities based on national origins had little relevancy.

Millions of White Americans also fled the cities for the suburbs. During the 1950s the suburbs grew six times faster than the cities, and by 1960 one-third of all Americans lived in the suburbs. That number had increased to more than half by 1990. The suburbs offered space, security, and privacy. In places like Levittown, New York, a suburb of mass-produced houses developed by William Levitt, a family could buy a two-bedroom home in 1950 on a 60- by 100-foot lot for $7,999, or about $58 a month. Where once a home in the country was the privilege of the rich, now average Americans could enjoy aspects of country life. But again, Americans did not have an equal opportunity to share in the suburbs. Developers often excluded African Americans and other racial minorities from the suburbs, and Jewish Americans tended at first to stay close to their urban roots.

The growth of the suburbs indicated a profound change in the nation, one with social and political consequences. The growth was fueled at least partially by the federal government. The Highway Act of 1956 appropriated $26 billion to construct 41,000 (later expanded to 42,500) miles of interstate highways. It took longer to complete and was more expensive than originally planned, but the act changed America. It made the suburbs easier to reach and encouraged urban flight. At the same time, money spent on interstates was money not spent on urban infrastructures. As Americans moved to the suburbs, city roads, bridges, railway systems, and subways declined. This decline added to the impulse to move. And over the years, cities—especially the inner cities—languished, victims of new priorities and different dreams.

Far more than cities, suburbs became a land of automobiles, and in the suburbs cars became as important as homes. Fathers drove to work, mothers drove their children to school and drove to shop for food, adolescents when they turned 16 drove because they could. They were people on wheels, part of a nation on wheels. The process gave rise to a land of drive-in theaters, gasoline service stations, mobile homes, multicar garages, and malls. Between 1952 and 1972 the number of automobiles on American highways doubled and then doubled again by the mid-1990s, and in the process pollution increased and mass transportation declined. Probably no politician who voted for the highway act would have predicted the revolutionary results of the legislation.

The suburbs also served as a melting pot for residents. In the 1950s and 1960s, the suburbs served as the destinations for Americans engaged in "White flight"—the children and grandchildren of the "new immigrants" joined their British, German, and Scandinavian predecessors in taking up homes outside the cities. Women shopped in neighborhood supermarkets, carpooled their children to Cub Scouts, Boy Scouts, Girl Scouts, and Little League games, and became active in the PTA. Children were thrown together in newly built public schools. Although the suburbs were lily White and Christian, they nevertheless encouraged assimilation and undermined the significance of national origins as a component of ethnic identity.

In addition to suburban homes and automobiles, American pop culture in the 1950s encouraged assimilation. Back in the 1920s, the rise of the radio and film industries had spawned mass popular culture, with tens of millions of Americans listening to the same programs, hearing the same advertisements, purchasing the same consumer products, watching the same movies, and tracking the lives of the same heroes and celebrities. With the advent of television and rock and roll in the 1950s, the power of mass culture expanded exponentially, bringing together Americans from all walks of life. Sports, music, television, and movies became the new cultural currency, and in the process the old ethnic language theaters, ethnic films, and ethnic publications declined. In the 1990s, the rise of the Internet created a new venue for pop culture assimilation. And as Americans consumed the same information and the same images, they gradually became more similar, and older ethnic differences, especially those based on national origins, blurred and became less distinct.

Educational achievement also worked to blur Old World identities. For several generations in America, ethnic Catholics had viewed economic success as an Anglo-American phenomenon, as if only White Protestants were eligible for progress and money. Ethnic Catholics often regarded public education as a threat to religion and community life, and they elevated hard work and blue-collar traditions to philosophical levels. Many Poles and Slovaks, for example, defined success not in social and economic terms but in the persistence of cultural and religions values. Hispanic writer Richard Rodriguez remembered growing up in southern California in the 1950s. "It mattered that education was changing me," he wrote. "It never ceased to matter. . . . 'Your parents must be very proud of you,' people began to say to me about the time I was in the sixth grade. To answer affirmatively, I'd smile. Shyly I'd smile, never betraying my sense of irony; I was not proud of my mother and father. I was embarrassed by their lack of education. . . . I heard my father speak to my teacher and felt ashamed of his labored, accented words. Then I felt guilty for the shame. I felt such contradictory feelings."

But the grandchildren and great-grandchildren of Roman Catholic immigrants felt less and less guilty about such feelings and began defining success in more material terms, placing a new premium on education and occupational achievement. By the 1990s, for example, Irish

Catholic educational levels and family income well exceeded the national averages, whereas those of Polish Americans, Slovak Americans, and Hungarian Americans had reached the national average. Among Romanian Americans, educational achievement and national income far exceeded the national average. Education encourages assimilation because it is a great leveler of ethnic identity. It reshapes perspectives, undermines traditions, and reorients individuals away from traditional institutions. Educated people become more willing and therefore more likely to discard racial and ethnic stereotypes, move away from old neighborhoods, establish new institutional loyalties, and interact with people from different ethnic and racial backgrounds.

Among the descendants of White immigrants—Protestants, Catholics, and Jews—the decline of the old neighborhoods of the urban Northeast and Midwest, the rise of the suburbs and the Sunbelt, the appearance of mass popular culture, and higher levels of education dramatically increased social and economic interaction among people from different ethnic backgrounds. Out of those new associations came higher rates of intermarriage. Among Americans of European descent, intermarriage rates accelerated. By 2000, for example, more than 80 percent of Irish Catholics and German Catholics married non-Irish and non-Germans, respectively, and the rates were 65 percent for Poles, Czechs, and Italians and 55 percent for French Canadians. Among American Protestants of European descent, for whom narrow national origin identities had lost much of their meaning, intermarriage rates were far higher.

At the end of World War II, more than 80 percent of Protestants, 84 percent of Roman Catholics, and 94 percent of Jews married within their religious commitments, prompting some sociologists to describe a "triple melting pot" in America—Protestants, Catholics, and Jews. If, for example, a young woman of Swedish Lutheran descent did not marry another Swedish Lutheran, she might marry a German Lutheran or an Episcopalian but only rarely a Roman Catholic. And if a Polish Catholic young man did not marry another Polish Catholic, he might marry an Irish Catholic or a German Catholic but only rarely a Protestant. A fourth religious melting pot appeared in the United States during the 1980s and 1990s. More than any other religious group in the country, Muslim immigrants married endogamously, selecting other Muslims as marriage partners more than 90 percent of the time.

By the year 2000, however, among Protestants, Catholics, and Jews, the triple melting pot was beginning to break down as the forces of assimilation blurred narrow religious identities. More than 60 percent of Jews married non-Jews, and nearly 60 percent of Roman Catholics were marrying non-Catholics. The intermarriage rate among Jews was so high that Jewish leaders worried about the long-term survival of a Jewish identity in the United States. One Jewish scholar wrote, "Younger Jews are not just overwhelmingly native born, they are native Americans, integrated into American society and as such more distant from public and civil Judaism and its more parochial manifestations of traditional observance and identity and even from ethnic or political connection to Israel. If they represent the future of Judaism in America, it is a future that is significantly less Jewishly intense and involved."

Along racial lines, intermarriage rates were substantially lower, but even then signs of change were appearing. The 2000 census counted a population of 2.3 million Native Americans in the United States, but less than 20 percent of them were "full-bloods"—individuals with two parents from one tribe. The rest were "mixed bloods"—with parents of mixed Indian heritage or various degrees of Indian, Mexican, and White ancestry. More than 50 percent of Japanese Americans and 50 percent of Puerto Rican Americans married non-Japanese and non-Puerto Ricans, respectively, and among Mexican Americans the inter-marriage rate was 40 percent. Among second-generation Chinese Americans in 2000, intermarriage rates exceeded 40 percent in Hawaii and Los Angeles, and were only slightly lower in New York City.

When Puerto Ricans did not marry other Puerto Ricans or Mexican Americans did not marry other Mexican Americans, more often than not they still married people from Hispanic backgrounds. Because they worked side by side in the large commercial farms of the Southwest, Filipino Americans and Mexican Americans had a high rate of intermarriage. In fact, a large Hispanic melting pot had appeared in the United States in the 1990s. When Cuban Americans did not marry other Cuban Americans, they usually married Puerto Ricans, Dominicans, Salvadorans, Nicaraguans, Hondurans, or Mexicans because of the language and religious bonds they shared as Spanish-speaking Roman Catholics. Most non-Hispanics tended to lump all Spanish-speaking people together, and marriage patterns, especially in immigrants and their children, followed suit. Of course, in regions where one ethnic group constituted a majority—such as Cuban Americans in Miami, Mexican Americans in Los Angeles, or Dominicans in the Corona-Jackson Heights section of Queens in New York City—members of those ethnic groups were far more likely to marry endogamously than not.

But in 2000 the forces of assimilation in the United States had still not managed to breach the color barrier, especially concerning African Americans. More than 95 percent of Americans of European descent married other Whites, and 95 percent of African Americans married other Blacks. When Whites did marry non-Whites, they were ten times more likely to select an Asian or Hispanic partner than a Black partner. The color line even had an impact on recent immigrants. When a Puerto Rican of African descent married a non-Puerto

Rican, the new wife or husband was far more likely to be an African American than a non-African Hispanic. The same was true for Afro-Cubans and Afro-Dominicans. When a Mexican American married a non-Mexican, non-Hispanic, the partner was far more likely to be White than Black. Although assimilation is breaking down language, national origins, and religious barriers, the racial barrier, especially for African Americans, remains rigid and entrenched.

To be sure, the obstacles are not as large as those faced by their ancestors. The number of African Americans holding public office is three times as high as it was in the mid–1960s, and in the 1970s, 1980s, and 1990s, Black household income rose at a slightly higher rate than White household income. The Black middle class today is twice as large as it was in 1970. But in 2000 Black unemployment was still twice that of Whites, and Black families were twice as likely to live below the poverty line than Whites. By the late 1990s, one of five Black men between the ages of 15 and 34 had a prison record, and Blacks constituted one-third of new AIDS cases, even though they made up only 12 percent of the population. Discrimination thrives, though it has moved underground, and Blacks still encounter formidable obstacles to success. In 1985, African American writer James Baldwin wrote, "The reality, the depth, and the persistence of the delusion of white supremacy in this country causes any real concept of education to be as remote, and as much to be feared, as change or freedom itself."

Today, approximately 5,000 immigrants arrived in the United States. Some came legally by train from Mexico, by car from Canada, and by air from around the world. They will work hard to support their families and will try to preserve elements of the Old World culture. Others arrived surreptitiously and illegally, on rickety boats from the Caribbean and the Florida Straits, by foot climbing fences and crossing the U.S.–Mexico border, or riding crammed into backs of trucks driven by "coyotes" who specialize in the immigrant trade. Some will claim political asylum, and others on travel or student visas will simply not return home and hope to find a way of staying permanently in the United States. The undocumented immigrants will melt into the streets of Miami, Los Angeles, New York City, Philadelphia, Houston, and dozens of other major cities and larger towns and spend years dodging border patrols and INS agents. Two to three generations from now, the descendants of these immigrants will lose the battle with the forces of assimilation and blend into American society. Collectively, legal or not, they will continue to do what immigrants have always done—to measure the true meaning of equality of opportunity and to infuse American culture with an ethic of hard work, a spirit of rebellion, a willingness to test new ideas, and an inclination to reinvent society.

BIBLIOGRAPHY

Alba, Richard D. *Ethnic Identity: The Transformation of White America.* New Haven, CT: Yale University Press, 1990.

Chan, Sucheng. *Asian Americans: An Interpretive History.* New York: Twayne, 1991.

Chavez, Linda. *Out of the Barrio: Toward a New Politics of Hispanic Assimilation.* New York: Basic Books, 1991.

Davis, Abraham L., and Barbara Luck Graham. *The Supreme Court, Race, and Civil Rights.* Thousand Oaks, CA: Sage, 1995.

Dinnerstein, Leonard. *Antisemitism in America.* New York: Oxford University Press, 1994.

Fitzgerald, Keith. *The Face of the Nation: Immigration, the State, and the National Identity.* Stanford, CA: Stanford University Press, 1996.

Formisano, Ronald. *Boston Against Busing: Race, Class, and Ethnicity in the 1960s and 1970s.* Chapel Hill: University of North Carolina Press, 1991.

Fugita, Stephen S., and David J. O'Brien. *Japanese American Ethnicity: The Persistence of Community.* Seattle: University of Washington Press, 1991.

Gabaccia, Donna. *From the Other Side: Women, Gender, and Immigrant Life in the U.S., 1820-1990.* Bloomington: Indiana University Press, 1994.

Gaines, Kevin. *Uplifting the Race: Black Leadership, Politics and Culture in the Twentieth Century.* Chapel Hill: University of North Carolina Press, 1986.

Garrow, David J. *Bearing the Cross: Martin Luther King, Jr., and the Southern Christian Leadership Conference, 1955-1968.* New York: William Morrow, 1986.

———. *Protest at Selma: Martin Luther King, Jr., and the Voting Rights Act of 1965.* New Haven, CT: Yale University Press, 1978.

Gómez-Quiñones, Juan. *Mexican-American Labor, 1790-1990.* Albuquerque: University of New Mexico Press, 1994.

Griswold Del Castillo, Richard, and Arnoldo de León. *North to Aztlán: A History of Mexican Americans in the United States.* New York: Twayne, 1996.

Gutiérrez, David G. *Walls and Mirrors: Mexican Americans, Mexican Immigrants, and the Politics of Ethnicity.* Berkeley: University of California Press, 1995.

Haddad, Yvonne. *Islamic Values in the United States: A Comparative Study.* New York: Oxford University Press, 1987.

Haddad, Yvonne Yazbeck, and Jane Idleman Smith. *Mission to America: Five Islamic Communities in North America*. Gainesville: University of Florida Press, 1993.

Hatamiya, Leslie T. *Righting a Wrong: Japanese Americans and the Passage of the Civil Liberties Act of 1988*. Stanford, CA: Stanford University Press, 1993.

Heilman, Samuel C. *Portrait of American Jews: The Last Half of the 20th Century*. Seattle: University of Washington Press, 1995.

Hein, Jeremy. *From Vietnam, Laos, and Cambodia: A Refugee Experience in the United States*. New York: Twayne, 1995.

Heinze, Andrew R. *Adapting to Abundance: Jewish Immigrants, Mass Consumption, and the Search for American Identity*. New York: Columbia University Press, 1990.

Helweg, Arthur M., and Usha M. Helweg. *An Immigrant Success Story: East Indians in America*. Philadelphia: University of Pennsylvania Press, 1990.

Hertzberg, Arthur. *The Jews in America: Four Centuries of an Uneasy Encounter*. New York: Simon & Schuster, 1989.

Jones, Maldwyn Allen. *American Immigration*, 2d ed. Chicago: University of Chicago Press, 1992.

Kasinitz, Philip. *Caribbean New York: Black Immigrants and the Politics of Race*. Ithaca, NY: Cornell University Press, 1992.

Kelley, Ron, ed. *IRANGELES: Iranians in Los Angeles*. Berkeley: University of California Press, 1993.

Kim, Hyuang-chan. *The Korean Diaspora*. Santa Barbara, CA: ABC-Clio, 1977.

King, Richard. *Civil Rights and the Idea of Freedom*. Athens: University of Georgia Press, 1996.

Lemann, Nicholas. *The Promised Land: The Great Black Migration and How It Changed America*. New York: Alfred A. Knopf, 1991.

Lessinger, Johanna. *From the Ganges to the Hudson: Indian Immigrants in New York City*. Boston: Allyn & Bacon, 1995.

Lyman, Stanford. *Color, Culture, and Civilization: Race and Minority Issues in American Society*. Urbana: University of Illinois Press, 1994.

Mahler, Sarah J. *Salvadorans in Suburbia: Symbiosis and Conflict*. Boston: Allyn & Bacon, 1995.

Mangione, Jerre, and Ben Morreale. *La Storia: Five Centuries of the Italian American Experience*. New York: HarperCollins, 1992.

Margolis, Maxine. *Little Brazil: An Ethnography of Brazilian Immigrants in New York City*. Princeton, NJ: Princeton University Press, 1994.

Min, Pyong Gap. *Caught in the Middle: Korean Merchants in America's Multiethnic Cities*. Berkeley: University of California Press, 1996.

Moore, Kathleen. *American Law and the Transformation of Muslim Life in the United States*. Albany: State University of New York Press, 1995.

Olson, James. *Catholic Immigrants in American History*. Chicago: Nelson Hall, 1987.

———. *The Ethnic Dimension in American History*. New York: St. Martin's, 1993.

―――. *Native Americans in the Twentieth Century.* Urbana: University of
Illinois Press, 1984.

Olson, James S., and Judith Olson. *Cuban Americans: From Tragedy to
Triumph.* New York: Twayne, 1995.

Palmer, Ransford W. *Pilgrims in the Sun: West Indian Migration to America.*
New York: Twayne, 1995.

Pessar, Patricia R. *A Visa for a Dream: Dominicans in the United States.*
Boston: Allyn & Bacon, 1995.

Pommershein, Frank. *Braid of Feathers: American Indian Law and
Contemporary Tribal Life.* Berkeley: University of California Press, 1995.

Pula, James S. *Polish Americans: An Ethnic Community.* New York: Twayne,
1995.

Reimers, David M. *Still the Golden Door: The Third World Comes to
America.* New York: Columbia University Press, 1992.

Repack, Terry A. *Waiting on Washington: Central American Workers in the
Nation's Capital.* Philadelphia: Temple University Press, 1995.

Rodríguez, Clara E. *Puerto Ricans: Born in the U.S.A.* Boulder, CO: Westview,
1989.

Roediger, David R. *The Wages of Whiteness: Race and the Making of the
American Working Class.* New York: Verso, 1991.

Rutledge, Paul James. *The Vietnamese Experience in the United States.*
Bloomington: Indiana University Press, 1992.

Small, Steven. *Racialised Barriers: The Black Experience in the United States
and England in the 1980s.* New York: Routledge, 1994.

Spickard, Paul. *Mixed Blood: Intermarriage and Ethnic Identity in
Twentieth-Century America.* Madison: University of Wisconsin Press,
1989.

Stavans, Ilan. *The Hispanic Condition: Reflections on Culture and Identity
in America.* New York: HarperCollins, 1995.

Sutter, Valerie O'Connor. *The Indochinese Refugee Dilemma.* Baton Rouge:
Louisiana State University Press, 1990.

Wearne, Phillip. *Return of the Indian: Conquest and Revival in the
Americas.* Philadelphia: Temple University Press, 1996.

Wei, William. *The Asian American Movement.* Philadelphia: Temple
University Press, 1993.

Wunder, John R. *"Retained by the People": A History of Americans and the
Bill of Rights.* New York: Oxford University Press, 1994.

Zephir, Flore. *Haitian Immigrants in Black America: A Sociological and
Sociolinguistic Portrait.* Westport, CT: Bergin & Garvey, 1996.

INDEX